Foreword

From the Chief of Staff of the Army

The Army Operating Concept (AOC) describes how future Army forces will prevent conflict, shape security environments, and win wars while operating as part of our Joint Force and working with multiple partners. The AOC guides future force development by identifying first order capabilities that the Army needs to support U.S. policy objectives. It provides the intellectual foundation and framework for learning and for applying what we learn to future force development under Force 2025 and Beyond.

The title, Win in a Complex World, emphasizes ready land forces' importance for protecting our nation and securing our vital interests against determined, elusive, and increasingly capable enemies. While the concept underscores the foundational capabilities the Army needs to prevent wars and shape security environments, it also recognizes that to deter enemies, reassure allies, and influence neutrals the Army must conduct sophisticated expeditionary maneuver and joint combined arms operations.

The AOC's vision of future armed conflict considers both continuities in war's nature and changes in its character. Conflicts in the future, like those in the past, will ultimately be resolved on land. Hence the concept recognizes that Army forces will be essential components of joint operations to create sustainable political outcomes while defeating enemies and adversaries who will challenge U.S. advantages in all domains: land, air, maritime, space, and cyberspace. Joint operations are critical to cope with such complexity, and the Army's contribution must provide unique capabilities and multiple options to the President, Secretary of Defense, and Combatant Commanders. These capabilities include tailorable and scalable combinations of special operations and conventional forces, regionally aligned and globally responsive combined arms teams, and foundational theater capabilities to enable joint operations. To do this, innovation is critical, both for the operational and the institutional Army, and the AOC is a beginning point for the innovation we need to ensure that our Soldiers, leaders, and teams are prepared to win in a complex world.

RAYMOND T. ODIERNO
General, United States Army
Chief of Staff

This page intentionally left blank

Preface

From the Commanding General
U.S. Army Training and Doctrine Command

One of our most important duties as Army professionals is to think clearly about the problem of future armed conflict. That is because our vision of the future must drive change to ensure that Army forces are prepared to prevent conflict, shape the security environment, and win wars. The purpose of the Army Operating Concept is to ask big questions, not focus on small answers. This concept focuses on three big questions; what level of war is the concept going to address, what is the environment we think Army forces will operate in, and what is the problem we are trying to solve.

This concept, for the first time, focuses on all three levels of war; tactical, operational, and strategic. The environment the Army will operate in is unknown. The enemy is unknown, the location is unknown, and the coalitions involved are unknown. The problem we are focusing on is how to "Win in a Complex World."

"Win" occurs at the strategic level and involves more than just firepower. It involves the application of all elements of National Power. Complex is defined as an environment that is not only unknown, but unknowable and constantly changing. The Army cannot predict who it will fight, where it will fight, and with what coalition it will fight. To win in a complex world, Army forces must provide the Joint Force with multiple options, integrate the efforts of multiple partners, operate across multiple domains, and present our enemies and adversaries with multiple dilemmas.

Multiple Dilemmas. The key to a Strategic Win is to present the enemy with multiple dilemmas. To compel enemy actions requires putting something of value to them at risk. Army forces allow joint force commanders to dictate the terms of operations and render enemies incapable of responding effectively. To present enemies and adversaries with multiple dilemmas, this concept introduces the idea of *Joint Combined Arms Operations*, an expansion of the traditional concept of combined arms to include the integration of not only joint capabilities, but also the broad range of efforts necessary to accomplish the mission. Joint combined arms operations allows joint force commanders to operate consistent with the tenet of *initiative*, dictating the terms of operations and rendering the enemy incapable of responding. Future forces operating as part of joint teams will conduct expeditionary maneuver through rapid deployment and transition to operations. Units possess the ability to operate dispersed over wide areas because they are able to integrate intelligence and operations to develop *situational understanding through action* while possessing the *mobility* to concentrate rapidly. Future forces conduct operations consistent with the tenet of *adaptability*, anticipating dangers and opportunities and adjusting operations to seize, retain, and exploit the initiative. Additionally, Army forces present the enemy with multiple dilemmas because they possess the *simultaneity* to overwhelm the enemy physically and psychologically, the *depth* to prevent enemy forces from recovering, and the *endurance* to sustain operations. Army forces are able to conduct joint combined arms operations because Soldiers, leaders, and teams thrive in environments of uncertainty and danger.

Multiple Options. This concept adds *set the theater* and *shape security environments* as core competencies to emphasize the Army's role in providing options to joint force commanders across the range of operations to include large scale combat operations, limited contingencies, security force assistance, humanitarian assistance, and disaster response. This concept also adds *special operations* as an Army core competency to highlight the Army's ability to provide dynamic combinations of conventional and unconventional forces. The concept calls for regionally engaged Army forces to establish a *global landpower network,* shape security environments, and prevent conflict. Although there are political costs and sensitivities associated with the employment of U.S. ground forces, the presence or arrival of credible Army forces demonstrates U.S. resolve and commitment to partners and adversaries. Army forces provide combatant commanders with the ability to compel outcomes without the cooperation of the enemy. It is for these reasons that this concept emphasizes the Army's ability to impose our nation's will on an enemy by force as essential to deterring war and preserving options short of war. This concept also emphasizes the Army's critical role in establishing stable environments to *consolidate gains* and achieve sustainable outcomes.

Multiple domains. Army operations are inherently cross-domain operations. U.S. forces depend on and complement joint efforts in the land, air, maritime, space, and cyberspace domains to enable operations on land. Because joint force freedom of movement and action across all domains are increasingly challenged by elusive land-based threats, this concept emphasizes Army operations to gain, sustain, and exploit control over land, to deny its use to the enemy. Future Army forces help ensure access through joint forcible entry operations with combined arms units that possess the mobility, firepower, and protection to defeat the enemy and establish control of land, resources, and populations. Future Army forces will support joint force freedom of movement and action through the projection of power from land across the maritime, air, space, and cyberspace domains. To assure allies, deter conflict, and compel determined and elusive enemies, the concept introduces a tenet of *simultaneity,* emphasizing the need for Army forces to extend efforts beyond the physical battleground to other contested spaces such as public perception, political subversion, and criminality.

Multiple partners. American military power is joint power. How combatant and joint force commanders combine land, air, maritime, space, and cyberspace capabilities gives U.S. forces a competitive advantage over enemies and adversaries. Army forces contribute to joint force mission accomplishment by providing *foundational* capabilities that permit effective integration of military, interorganizational, and multinational efforts. It is the need to integrate these efforts of multiple partners on land, in contested and dangerous environments and in response to crises in the homeland or overseas, which requires Army forces to integrate the efforts of others and *project national power*.

Developing the Future Force. The Army Operating Concept is the start point for developing the future force. As the historian Sir Michael Howard observed, "No matter how clearly one thinks, it is impossible to anticipate precisely the character of future conflict. The key is to not be so far off the mark that it becomes impossible to adjust once that character is revealed." The tenet of *innovation* challenges us to anticipate changing conditions to ensure that Army forces are manned, trained, and equipped to overmatch enemies in order to seize, retain, and exploit the initiative. We must not be consumed with focusing solely on avoiding risk, but build leaders and institutions that recognize and leverage opportunities. Leaders at all levels must encourage prudent risk taking and not allow bureaucratic processes to stifle them. Finally, we must assess our efforts continuously and be prepared to adapt to unexpected opportunities and unanticipated dangers. Our Army must continuously learn, adapt, and innovate. The tenets in this concept must apply to the institutional Army as well as the operational Army.

DAVID G. PERKINS
General, U.S. Army
Commanding

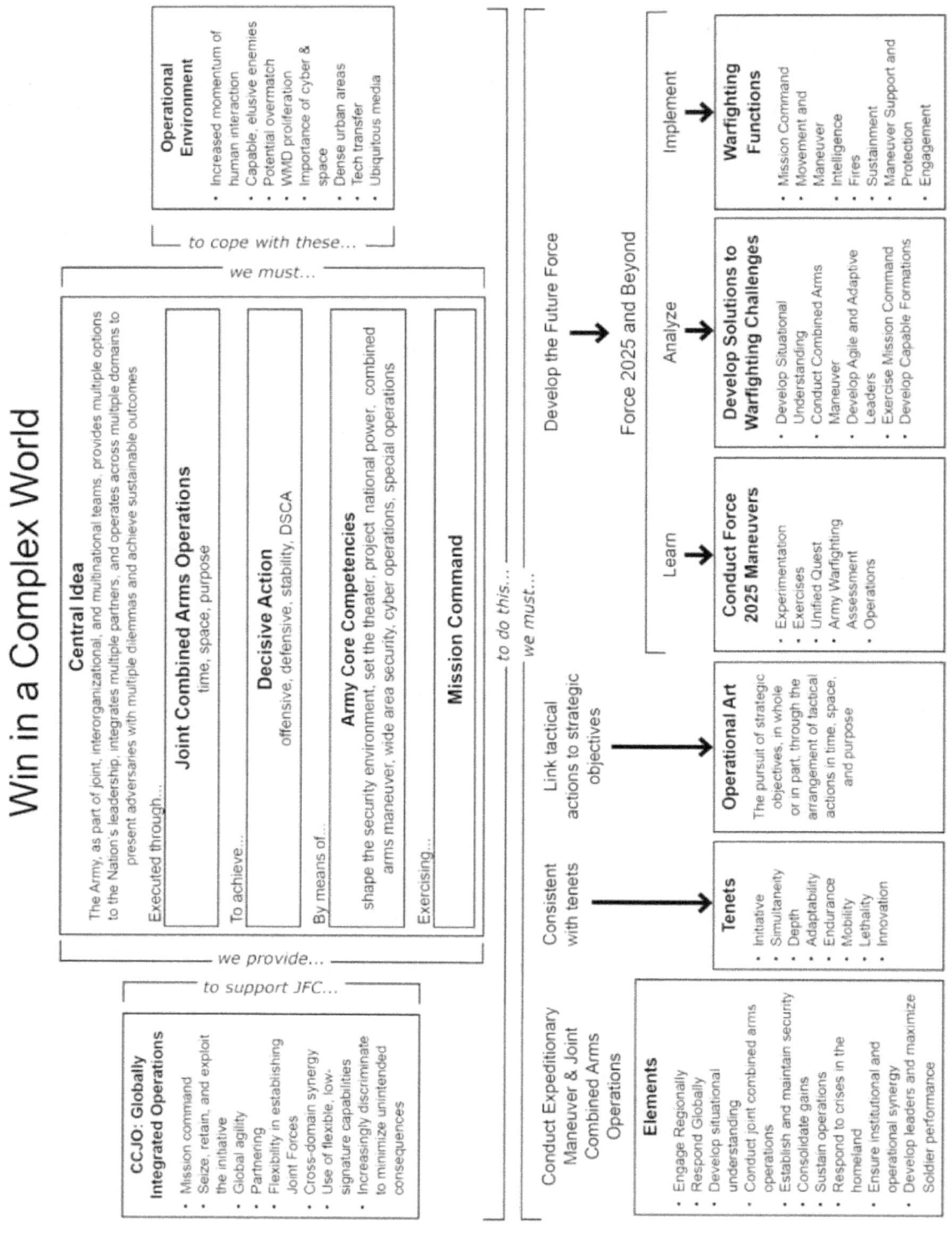

Figure 1. Win in a complex world logic chart

Department of the Army
Headquarters, United States Army
Training and Doctrine Command
Fort Eustis, VA 23604

7 October 2014

TRADOC Pamphlet 525-3-1*

Military Operations

THE U.S. ARMY OPERATING CONCEPT: WIN IN A COMPLEX WORLD

DAVID G. PERKINS
General, U.S. Army
Commanding

RICHARD D. MONTIETH
Colonel, GS
Deputy Chief of Staff, G-6

History. This is a major revision to U.S. Army Training and Doctrine Command (TRADOC) Pamphlet 525-3-1, The U.S. Army Operating Concept.

Summary. TRADOC Pamphlet 525-3-1 describes how future Army forces, as part of joint, interorganizational, and multinational efforts, operate to accomplish campaign objectives and protect U.S. national interests. It describes the Army's contribution to globally integrated operations, and addresses the need for Army forces to provide foundational capabilities for the Joint Force and to project power onto land and from land across the air, maritime, space, and cyberspace domains. The Army Operating Concept guides future force development through the identification of first order capabilities that the Army must possess to accomplish missions in support of policy goals and objectives.

Applicability. This concept applies to all Department of the Army (DA) activities that develop doctrine, organizations, training, materiel, leadership and education, personnel, and facilities (DOTMLPF) capabilities. This concept guides future force development and informs subsequent supporting concepts and the Joint Capabilities Integration and Development System (JCIDS) process. It also supports Army capabilities development processes described in TRADOC Regulation 71-20 and functions as a conceptual basis for developing subordinate concepts related to the future force within DOTMLPF.

*This pamphlet supersedes TRADOC Pamphlet 525-3-1, dated 19 August 2010.

Proponent and supplementation authority. The proponent for this pamphlet is the Director, Army Capabilities Integration Center (ARCIC). The proponent has the authority to approve exceptions or waivers to this pamphlet that are consistent with controlling law and regulations. Do not supplement this pamphlet without prior approval from Director, ARCIC (ATFC-ED), 950 Jefferson Avenue, Fort Eustis, VA 23604.

Suggested improvements. Users are invited to submit comments and suggested improvements using DA Form 2028 (Recommended Changes to Publications and Blank Forms) to Director, ARCIC (ATFC-ED), 950 Jefferson Avenue, Fort Eustis, VA 23604. Suggested improvements may also be submitted using DA Form 1045 (Army Ideas for Excellence Program Proposal).

Availability. This TRADOC pamphlet is available only on the TRADOC homepage at http://www.tradoc.army.mil/tpubs/.

Summary of Change

TRADOC Pamphlet 525-3-1
The U.S. Army Operating Concept: Win in a Complex World

This revision, dated 7 October 2014-

o Updates the title, problem statement, and central idea (title changed throughout and sections 3-1. [problem statement], 3-2. [central idea]).

o Emphasizes the human aspects of armed conflict (throughout).

o Describes how Army forces conduct joint combined arms operations as part of globally integrated operations consistent with the Capstone Concept for Joint Operations: Joint Force 2020 and United States Army Training and Doctrine Command Pamphlet 525-3-0, The U.S. Army Capstone Concept (throughout).

o Provides an updated operational context for the Army's roles and missions (chapter 2).

o Refines tenets and core competencies for the future Army (section 3-4.).

o Updates required capabilities and describes how the Army will develop the future force (appendix B).

o Identifies science and technology priorities and emphasizes integration of skilled Soldiers and teams with technology (appendix C).

o Identifies risks associated with adopting this concept and ways to mitigate risks (appendix D).

Contents

This page intentionally left blank

Chapter 1
Introduction

1-1. Purpose
United States (U.S.) Army Training and Doctrine Command (TRADOC) Pamphlet (TP) 525-3-1, The U.S. Army Operating Concept (AOC): Win in a Complex World, describes how future Army forces, as part of joint, interorganizational,[1] and multinational efforts, operate to accomplish campaign objectives and protect U.S. national interests.[2] It describes the Army's contribution to globally integrated operations, which is the central idea of the *Capstone Concept for Joint Operations: Joint Force 2020.* The AOC recognizes the need for Army forces to provide foundational capabilities required by the Joint Force and to project power onto land and from land across the air, maritime, space, and cyberspace domains.[3] The AOC is grounded in a vision of future armed conflict that considers national defense strategy; missions; emerging operational environments; advances in technology; and anticipated enemy, threat, and adversary capabilities.[4] Ultimately, the AOC guides future force development through the identification of first order capabilities that the Army must possess to accomplish missions in support of policy goals and objectives.[5]

1-2. References
Appendix A lists required and related publications.

1-3. Explanation of abbreviations and terms
The glossary explains abbreviations and special terms used in this pamphlet.

1-4. Relationship between Army doctrine and concepts

a. Doctrine explains how current Army forces operate and guides leaders and Soldiers in the conduct of training and operations. However, doctrine is not prescriptive and is not a substitute for creative thought or initiative.

b. Concepts describe how commanders might employ future capabilities against anticipated threats to accomplish missions. Concepts establish the intellectual foundation for Army modernization and help Army leaders identify opportunities to improve future force capabilities. The AOC guides the development of detailed concepts that address each of the Army's warfighting functions. The seven functional concepts are mission command, movement and maneuver, intelligence, fires, sustainment, engagement, and maneuver support and protection. The AOC is particularly important because it discusses how capabilities associated with warfighting functions *combine* in the conduct of joint operations.

c. Joint operations. Army forces conduct expeditionary operations consistent with the *Joint Operational Access Concept* and the *Joint Concept for Entry Operations.* Army combined arms teams integrate with other services and mission partners to conduct joint combined arms maneuver, the synchronized application of capabilities critical to accomplish the mission. Army forces, positioned forward or deployed rapidly from the United States, respond to and resolve crises, defeat enemies, establish security, and consolidate gains. Army forces are critical to projecting national power onto land as well as projecting military power from land across the air, maritime, space, and cyberspace domains.[6] Army forces possess the endurance and staying power to achieve sustainable outcomes.

1-5. Assumptions

a. The following assumptions about the future underpin the AOC:

(1) The U.S. Army will remain a professional, all-volunteer force, relying on all components of the Army to meet future commitments.[7]

(2) The Army will adjust to fiscal constraints and have resources sufficient to preserve the balance of readiness, force structure, and modernization necessary to meet the demands of the national defense strategy in the mid- to far-term (2020 to 2040).

(3) Army forces remain engaged overseas in areas vital to U.S. security interests, but a larger percentage of the force will be based in the continental United States.

(4) The land, air, maritime, space, and cyberspace domains will become more contested as U.S. military technological advantages decrease.

(5) Changes in technology and geopolitical dynamics as well as the enduring political and human nature of war will keep war in the realms of complexity and uncertainty.[8]

(6) Except for an immediate response to a national emergency, the Army will conduct operations as part of joint, interorganizational, and multinational teams.

b. The Army will continue to assess these assumptions.

Chapter 2
Operational Context

2-1. Introduction: Continuity and change in armed conflict

a. Anticipating the demands of future armed conflict requires an understanding of continuities in the nature of war as well as an appreciation for changes in the character of armed conflict. Technological advances and changes in strategic guidance, joint operating concepts, and security challenges require the U.S. Army to innovate to ensure that forces are prepared to accomplish future missions. Shifts in the geopolitical landscape caused by competition for power and resources influence the character of armed conflict. These shifts, and violence associated with them, occur more rapidly than in the past due to advances in technology, the proliferation of information, and the associated increased momentum of human interaction.[9]

b. Recent and ongoing conflicts reinforce the need to balance the technological focus of Army modernization with a recognition of the limits of technology and an emphasis on the human, cultural, and political continuities of armed conflict. Nations and organizations in the future will fight for the same reasons that the Greek historian Thucydides identified 2,500 years ago: fear, honor, and interest.[10] Every armed conflict exhibits some combination of violence, emotion, policy, chance, and risk. Fundamentally, war will remain a contest of wills.[11] Although advances in technology will continue to influence the character of warfare, the effect of technologies on land are often not as great as in other domains due to geography, the interaction with adaptive enemies, the presence of noncombatants, and other complexities associated with war's continuities.

c. Threats to U.S. vital interests across the land, air, maritime, space, and cyberspace domains originate on land. Land-based threats emanate from the fielded forces of hostile nation states and from areas where state weakness allows nonstate enemy or adversary organizations to operate. Conflict often arises from disorder (the breakdown of peaceful and lawful behavior). In conflicts involving nation states, disorder often follows the defeat of enemy forces or the collapse of a regime. Land forces are required to overcome the effects of this disorder through military operations that integrate joint, interorganizational, and multinational capabilities. Although the ability to project power onto land from the air, maritime, space, and cyberspace domains will remain vital to joint operations, the employment of land forces will remain essential to achieve political outcomes.

d. The character of future warfare evolves based upon assigned missions; the operational environment; emerging technologies; and changes in enemy capabilities, objectives, and will. The Army must anticipate change while considering how continuities, such as those reflected in the principles of war, affect how the Army must operate to accomplish future missions.[12]

2-2. The Army's missions and contributions to joint operations

a. The 2014 Quadrennial Defense Review identified eleven enduring Armed Forces missions in which the Army plays a substantial role:[13]
- Provide for military defense of the homeland.
- Defeat an adversary.
- Provide a global stabilizing presence.
- Combat terrorism.
- Counter weapons of mass destruction (WMD).
- Deny an adversary's objectives.
- Respond to crisis and conduct limited contingency operations.
- Conduct military engagement and security cooperation.
- Conduct stability and counterinsurgency operations.
- Provide support to civil authorities.
- Conduct humanitarian assistance and disaster response.

b. These missions are consistent with the Army's long-standing role in national defense. The Army must remain prepared to protect the homeland, foster security globally, project power, and win. To protect the homeland, the Army deters and defeats attacks and mitigates the effects of attacks and natural disasters. To foster security, the Army engages regionally and prepares to respond globally to compel enemies and adversaries. To project power and win decisively, the

Army, as the Nation's principal land force, organizes, trains, and equips forces for prompt and sustained combat on land.

c. Army forces in joint operations. American military power is joint power. The Army both depends on and supports air and naval forces across the land, air, maritime, space, and cyberspace domains. The Army depends on the other services for strategic and operational mobility, fires, close air support, and other capabilities. The Army supports other services, combatant commands, multinational forces, and interorganizational partners with foundational capabilities such as communications, intelligence, rotary wing aviation, missile defense, logistics, and engineering.[14] Army forces are uniquely suited to shape security environments through forward presence and sustained engagements with allied and partner land forces. Army forces defeat enemy land forces and seize, hold, and defend land areas. The Army also prepares for security operations abroad including initial establishment of military government pending transfer of this responsibility to other authorities.[15] Balanced Joint Force capabilities create synergy and provide the President, Secretary of Defense, and combatant commanders with multiple options to prevent conflict, shape security environments, and win wars.

d. The AOC describes how Army forces operating as part of joint, interorganizational, and multinational teams accomplish the mission and win in a complex world. Army forces are prepared to do more than fight and defeat enemies; they must possess the capability to translate military objectives into enduring political outcomes. Army forces must have the capability (ability to achieve a desired effect under specified standards and conditions) and capacity (capability with sufficient scale and endurance) to accomplish assigned missions while confronting increasingly dangerous threats in complex operational environments.[16]

2-3. Anticipated threats and the future operational environment

a. Diverse enemies will employ traditional, unconventional, and hybrid strategies to threaten U.S. security and vital interests. Threats may emanate from nation states or nonstate actors such as transnational terrorists, insurgents, and criminal organizations. Enemies will continue to apply advanced as well as simple and dual-use technologies (such as improvised explosive devices). Enemies *avoid* U.S. strengths (such as long-range surveillance and precision strike) through traditional countermeasures (such as dispersion, concealment, and intermingling with civilian populations). As new military technologies are more easily transferred, potential threats *emulate* U.S. military capabilities to counter U.S. power projection and limit U.S. freedom of action. These capabilities include precision-guided rockets, artillery, mortars, and missiles that target traditional U.S. strengths in the air and maritime domains. Hostile nation states may attempt to overwhelm defense systems and impose a high cost on the United States to intervene in a contingency or crisis.[17] State and nonstate actors apply technology to *disrupt* U.S. advantages in communications, long-range precision fires, and surveillance. Enemy actions reduce U.S. ability to achieve dominance in the land, air, maritime, space, and cyberspace domains. Additionally, to accomplish political objectives, enemy organizations *expand* operations to the U.S. homeland. Enemies and adversaries will operate beyond physical battlegrounds and enemies will subvert efforts through infiltration of U.S. and partner forces (e.g., insider threat) while using propaganda and disinformation to effect public perception.

Paradoxically, the connectedness of networked devices within the U.S. presents adversaries with exploitable vulnerabilities.

b. The following five characteristics of the future operational environment are likely to have significant impact on land force operations.

(1) *Increased velocity and momentum of human interaction and events.* The speed at which information diffuses globally through multiple means increases the velocity, momentum, and degree of interaction among people. The diffusion of information via the Internet and social media amplifies and accelerates interaction between people, governments, militaries, and threats. Access to information allows organizations to mobilize people and resources locally, regionally, and globally. Disinformation and propaganda drive violence in support of political objectives. The compression of events in time requires forces capable of responding rapidly in sufficient scale to seize the initiative, control the narrative, and consolidate order.

(2) *Potential for overmatch.* Overmatch is the application of capabilities or use of tactics in a way that renders an adversary unable to respond effectively. Potential enemies invest in technologies to obtain a differential advantage and undermine U.S. ability to achieve overmatch.[18] These technologies include long-range precision fires, air defense systems, electric fires, and unmanned aerial systems (UAS). Anti-access and area denial capabilities challenge the Joint Force's ability to achieve air dominance and sea control as well as its ability to project power onto land from the air and maritime domains.[19] Potential enemies develop cyberspace capabilities such as disruptive and destructive malware and space capabilities such as anti-satellite weapons to disrupt U.S. communications and freedom of maneuver. To prevent enemy overmatch, the Army must develop new capabilities while anticipating enemy efforts to emulate or disrupt those capabilities. To retain overmatch, the Joint Force will have to combine technologies and integrate efforts across multiple domains to present enemies with multiple dilemmas.

(3) *Proliferation of weapons of mass destruction.* WMD proliferation to diverse state and nonstate actors in the form of chemical, biological, radiological, nuclear, and high-yield explosive (CBRNE) weapons poses an increased threat to U.S. and international security.[20] Adversaries share CBRNE knowledge, technology, and materiel. The risk of a nation losing control over nuclear assets increases as extremist organizations incite civil wars and establish control of territories, populations, and weapons. Moreover, directed energy and sophisticated CBRNE weapons could give adversaries unprecedented capabilities to threaten U.S. forces and civilian populations with mass casualties. Coping with CBRNE threats requires specially trained, equipped, and organized Army forces that have the ability to operate in inhospitable conditions, conduct reconnaissance to confirm or deny the presence of weapons, destroy enemy forces that possess those weapons, and secure territory to contain those weapons until CBRNE units reduce or neutralize them.

(4) *Spread of advanced cyberspace and counter-space capabilities.* The cyberspace and space domains grow in importance as global and regional competitors as well as nonstate actors invest in capabilities to protect their access and disrupt or deny access to others.[21] A broad array of actors challenges the Joint Force's freedom of action in space and cyberspace. Enemies and

adversaries collaborate as contests in space and cyberspace extend to and affect tactical operations. For example, enemy global positioning satellite jamming capabilities could render precision fires inaccurate. Army commanders must protect their own systems and disrupt the enemy's ability to operate. Army units will have to operate with degraded communications and reduced access to cyber and space capabilities. Army forces will have to support joint operations through reconnaissance, offensive operations or raids to destroy land-based enemy space and cyberspace capabilities.

(5) *Demographics and operations among populations, in cities, and in complex terrain.* The percentage of the world's population in urban areas will rise to sixty percent by 2030.[22] Internal migration and higher birth rates contribute to increasing urbanization.[23] Adversaries operate among the people in these urban areas and other complex terrain to avoid U.S. military advantages and they operate in cities because war, as a political phenomenon, is inherently about people. As cities grow, many governments fail to provide adequate security, employment, infrastructure, and services. Armed groups will exploit popular disaffection and weak governance. Urban areas become safe havens and support bases for terrorists, insurgents, or criminal organizations. Urban areas are potential scenes for mass atrocities. Enemies may use cities as launching platforms for long-range missiles that threaten allied as well as U.S. populations. Because urban environments degrade the ability to target threats with precision, joint operations will require land forces capable of operating in congested and restricted urban terrain (to include subsurface, surface, supersurface) to defeat those threats.[24] Understanding the technological, geographic, political, and military challenges of the urban environment will require innovative, adaptive leaders and cohesive teams who thrive in complex and uncertain environments. Operating in urban environments will require decentralized combined arms and joint capabilities.

2-4. Harbingers of future conflict

a. While the United States must assess new and emerging threats, many current operational challenges will exist into the future. Harbingers of future conflict include competing powers (e.g., China and Russia), regional powers (e.g., Iran and the Democratic People's Republic of Korea (DPRK)), transnational terrorist networks (e.g., al Qaida, its affiliates, and transnational criminals), and cyber threats.[25] The following are examples only and illustrate a limited number of threats for which future Army forces must prepare.

b. Competing powers.

(1) Though the People's Republic of China remains committed to stable relationships with neighbors and the U.S. in the near-term, it continues to pursue a long-term, comprehensive military modernization program designed to improve the capacity of its armed forces to fight and win short-duration, high-intensity regional contingencies.[26] China's goal over time is to expand its influence to establish stability along its periphery.[27] While China prefers to avoid direct confrontation with the U.S., it uses civilian assets to challenge actions such as U.S. surveillance flights. Moreover, China's behavior has created friction with regional neighbors including U.S. allies and partners.[28] Territorial disputes with Japan over the Senkaku/Diaoyu islands; border disputes with India; and increased maritime pressure on the Philippines, Malaysia, Taiwan, and

Vietnam are examples of China exerting power through force or threat of force.[29] China works to negate U.S. advantages in space and cyberspace. China is developing significant anti-satellite capabilities, integrating cyber into all aspects of military operations, and developing sophisticated missiles and air defenses as part of an effort to challenge United States' ability to project power. Chinese doctrine calls for combining conventional and unconventional actions.[30] The People's Liberation Army opened six combat training centers where it emphasizes combined arms operations and joint training.[31] Chinese actions and force modernization efforts highlight the need for Army forces positioned forward or regionally engaged to prevent conflict, deter adversaries, and strengthen partners. Emerging Chinese capabilities also highlight the need for Army forces to project power from land into the air, maritime, space, and cyberspace domains.

(2)   Russian annexation of the Crimean Peninsula and use of conventional and unconventional land forces in Ukraine suggest that Russia is determined to expand its territory and assert its power on the Eurasian landmass. Russia deployed and integrated a range of diplomatic, information, military, and economic means to conduct what some analysts have described as "non-linear" operations.[32] Russia conducted operations to pursue its war aims below the threshold that would elicit a concerted North Atlantic Treaty Organization response. In addition, Russia used cyberspace capabilities and social media to influence perceptions at home and abroad and provide cover for large-scale military operations. While the long-term results of the incursion into Ukraine are not yet certain, Russia demonstrated the centrality of land forces in its effort to assert power and advance its interests in former Soviet states. Without a viable land force capable of opposing the Russian army and its irregular proxies, such adventurism is likely to continue undeterred.[33] Russia's actions highlight the value of land forces to deter conflict as well as special operations and conventional force capability to project national power and exert influence in political contests.

c. Regional powers.

(1) Iran's management of its nuclear aspirations will shape its role as a rising power in the Middle East.[34] Iran, empowered by expanding sectarian conflicts in the greater Middle East, poses a hybrid threat to U.S. interests and allies in the region. As it continues to apply pressure on the region to erode and supplant U.S. power, Iran uses combinations of economic and diplomatic overtures with irregular forces to advance its interests. Iran develops partnerships with disenfranchised populations, religious factions, and criminal elements to create disorder focused on subverting the influence of the U.S. and partner nations. Iran also develops relationships with weak governments and uses those governments to advance its interests. For example, Iran's support for President Bashar al Assad in Syria is critical to its ability to sustain Lebanese Hezbollah, and Iran's support for militias in Iraq undermines government legitimacy and intensifies sectarian conflict.[35] Iran avoids direct military confrontations while developing advanced capabilities and pursuing comprehensive military modernization. Iran's modernization efforts include the use of automated systems on land, sea, and air; ballistic missiles; and the development of nuclear capability. Iran is actively supporting militia in Iraq while confronting the Islamic State in Iraq and the Levant (ISIL). Iran has become a more capable cyber actor as well. Taken collectively, Iranian activity has the potential to undermine U.S. regional goals as it continues to confront the U.S. indirectly on a number of fronts. Iran's hybrid armed forces

highlight the need for Army forces to remain effective against the fielded forces of nation states as well as networked guerilla and insurgent organizations.

(2) The DPRK, while in the same category as Iran, is at once a dangerous military threat and a failing state dependent upon the patronage of others, especially China. The DPRK is expanding its nuclear arsenal and improving its ballistic missile force to complement an aging but still large and capable conventional force. The DPRK's military possesses cyber and chemical-biological warfare capabilities. Key government facilities, military installations, and weapons are located in underground shelters. Because economic, social, and political pressures on the DPRK leadership could lead to war or a collapse of the regime, the U.S. prepares for the deployment of substantial ground, air, and maritime forces to operate as part of a coalition alongside Republic of Korea (South Korea) forces and in defense of South Korea. The threat on the Korean peninsula highlights the need for Army forces to operate in a CBRNE environment.

d. Transnational terrorist organizations. The emergence of ISIL is an example of how nonstate actors seize upon opportunities created by communal conflict and weak governance. ISIL is a nonstate actor that aims to create an Islamist militant state across large portions of Iraq, Syria, and surrounding areas. ISIL's military organization; ideological base; willingness to use murder and other forms of brutality against innocents; and ability to mobilize people, money, and weapons have enabled it to seize territory and establish control of populations and resources. ISIL exploits political opposition to governments to form alliances of convenience while acting to consolidate gains and marginalize competing insurgent groups through intimidation and coercion. ISIL moves into weakly governed spaces such as the Iraq-Syrian border where governments are unable to project power. These areas provide sanctuary and "strategic depth." ISIL uses social media and cyberspace to prosecute a propaganda campaign while using terrorist tactics (such as covert action, assassinations, destruction of historically significant property, extortion, and mass murder) to control populations and territory. The wider problem is ISIL's success combined with weaknesses of Middle Eastern governments has caused extremist Islam and terrorism to metastasize across much of the Middle East and North Africa. From Egypt to Yemen and from the Syrian Civil War to the disaster of Libya, the region is rife with weak governments and active terrorist groups. ISIL demonstrates the need for land forces to defeat determined enemies that operate among and control civilian populations. ISIL also highlights the need to extend efforts beyond physical battlegrounds to other contested spaces such as public perception and political subversion.

e. Transnational criminal organizations. Recent waves of migration from Central America to the U.S. – largely due to criminal violence – highlight second and third order threats to U.S. interests caused by transnational organized crime and weak governance. Ineffective governance provides an inviting environment for criminal organizations. Murders, kidnappings, and maimings in Central America equal or exceed violence associated with many political insurgencies in the Middle East and elsewhere. The region's militaries are engaged in support of law enforcement activities due to the severity of the problem and the inability of sometimes-corrupt police forces to cope with the problem. Criminal violence erodes state institutions and undermines governance. The threat from transnational organized crime highlights the need for Army special operations and regionally aligned forces to understand complex environments, operate with multiple partners, and conduct security force assistance.

2-5. Technologies with military application

a. Emerging technologies hold promise for improving future force combat effectiveness. Because of the ease with which many technological advantages are copied or countered, the Army must emphasize how to combine multiple technological improvements and counter enemy efforts to adopt or disrupt new technologies. (See appendix C for additional detail on technologies.) The U.S. Army's differential advantage over enemies derives, in part, from the integration of advanced technologies with skilled Soldiers and well-trained teams. These technologies and their potential to improve Army effectiveness include:

(1) Human and cognitive sciences may revolutionize the way the Army recruits, educates, trains, and develops leaders and Soldiers.

(2) Communications and information processing technology may improve understanding through common operational pictures and a reduction of technological complexity for users.

(3) New materials may deliver greater protection at lighter weights.

(4) Power saving and generation technologies may reduce sustainment demand and strategic lift requirements.

(5) Improved range, lethality, and precision of surface-to-air, air-to-surface, and surface-to-surface fires may help overcome anti-access and area denial challenges, extend mutual support across long distances, and permit land forces to project power into the air and maritime domains.

(6) Autonomous and semi-autonomous operational capabilities may increase lethality, improve protection, and extend Soldiers' and units' reach.

(7) Vertical take-off and landing aircraft combined with increased capabilities of UAS may provide a maneuver advantage for Army forces to overcome challenges of restrictive terrain and operations across long distances.

b. The technologies mentioned above are not all inclusive and may change as science and technological innovations grow and mature.

2-6. Conclusion

a. Future armed conflict will be complex, in part, because threats, enemies, and adversaries are becoming increasingly capable and elusive. State and nonstate actors employ traditional, unconventional, and hybrid strategies that threaten U.S. security and vital interests. The complexity of future armed conflict is due to increasing momentum of human interaction, threats emanating from dense and weakly governed urban areas, the availability of lethal weapon systems, and the proliferation of CBRNE threats. Enemies and adversaries will challenge U.S. competitive advantages in the land, air, maritime, space, and cyberspace domains. Advanced technologies will transfer readily to state and nonstate actors. Enemies possess the capability to threaten the U.S. homeland and project power from land into all other domains. Because these threats may originate in dense urban areas or remote safe havens, long-range strikes will prove insufficient to defeat them. The complexity of future armed conflict, therefore, will require Army forces capable of conducting missions in the homeland or in foreign lands including defense support of civil authorities, international disaster relief and humanitarian assistance, security cooperation activities, crisis response, or large-scale operations. What all Army operations will have in common is a need for innovative and adaptive leaders and cohesive teams that thrive in conditions of complexity and uncertainty.

b. The diversity of threats to U.S. security and vital interests will increase the need for Army forces to prevent conflict and shape security environments. Army forces have long been essential to preventing conflict through the forward positioning or rotation of forces overseas. Regionally engaged Army forces are needed to build partner capability, assure allies, and deter adversaries. While long-range strike and offshore capabilities will remain important to joint force operations, deterring threats from extended distance through retaliation often proves insufficient because determined adversaries attempt to achieve objectives rapidly at low cost prior to a U.S. or allied response. Army forces communicate U.S. commitment. Army forces and their partners bolster forward defense to dissuade adversaries who are unwilling to risk direct confrontation. Moreover, Army forces are critical to deterring conflict because they are capable of compelling outcomes without the cooperation of the enemy.

c. Compelling sustainable outcomes in war requires land forces to defeat enemy organizations, establish security, and consolidate gains. The Joint Force requires the Army to deploy credible and reliable combined arms capabilities across the range of military operations. In the complex future operating environment and while operating against hybrid enemies, Army forces will be essential for projecting national power through support for diplomatic, political, law enforcement, development, and other efforts.

d. Since World War II the prosperity and security of the United States have depended, in large measure, on the synergistic effects of capable land, air, and maritime forces. They have reinforced one another in the conduct of joint operations and together provided options that any one or two services could not provide alone. U.S. military power is joint power. Trends in threats, the operating environment, and technology highlight the enduring need for ready Army forces operating as part of joint, interorganizational, and multinational teams to prevent conflict, shape security environments, and win in a complex world.

Chapter 3
How Future Army Forces Operate

3-1. Military problem
To meet the demands of the future strategic environment in 2025 and beyond, how does the Army conduct joint operations promptly, in sufficient scale, and for ample duration to prevent conflict, shape security environments, and win wars?

3-2. Central idea

The Army, as part of joint, interorganizational, and multinational teams, protects the homeland and engages regionally to prevent conflict, shape security environments, and create multiple options for responding to and resolving crises. When called upon, globally responsive combined arms teams maneuver from multiple locations and domains to present multiple dilemmas to the enemy, limit enemy options, avoid enemy strengths, and attack enemy weaknesses. Forces tailored rapidly to the mission will exercise mission command and integrate joint, interorganizational, and multinational capabilities. Army forces adapt continuously to seize, retain, and exploit the initiative. Army forces defeat enemy organizations, control terrain, secure populations, consolidate gains, and preserve joint force freedom of movement and action in the land, air, maritime, space, and cyberspace domains.

3-3. How the Army operates

a. *Engage regionally.* Army forces engage regionally to ensure interoperability, build relationships based on common interests, enhance situational awareness, assure partners, and deter adversaries. Because threats starting at low levels often gain strength and become more dangerous over time,[36] Army forces engaged regionally are essential to the defense policy goals of shaping security environments and preventing conflict.[37] To promote regional security, Army special operations forces and regionally aligned conventional forces engage in a broad range of theater security cooperation activities including security force assistance. These activities are special operations forces-specific, special operations forces-centric, or conventional force-centric depending on the nature of the mission. When needed, Army forces reinforce or bolster the efforts of partners. Army units tailored to the mission provide advice as well as access to combined joint and Army capabilities. Army Reserve and Army National Guard units sustain long-term relationships and apply their unique civil-military expertise across military, government, economic, and social spheres. Conventional and special operations forces contribute to a global land network of relationships resulting in early warning, indigenous solutions, and informed campaigns. Regional engagement sets favorable conditions for a commitment of forces if diplomacy and deterrence fail.

b. *Respond globally.* Forward positioned and rotational forces demonstrate U.S. resolve and provide foundational capabilities to the Joint Force such as communications, intelligence, rotary wing aviation, missile defense, logistics, engineering, and expeditionary joint task force headquarters. Those capabilities combined with strategic airlift and sealift and prepositioned equipment on land or afloat ensure Army forces are prepared to deter adversaries; respond rapidly to crises; and conduct expeditionary maneuver against enemy forces that threaten U.S. interests.[38] Expeditionary maneuver, the rapid deployment of task organized combined arms forces able to transition quickly and conduct operations of sufficient scale and ample duration to achieve strategic objectives, aims to turn the enemy out of prepared positions or envelop forces from unexpected directions. Army forcible and early entry forces, protected by joint air and missile defense, achieve surprise and bypass or overcome enemy anti-access and area denial capabilities through intertheater and intratheater maneuver to multiple locations. Integrated special operations forces and combined arms teams dynamically task-organized for the mission conduct reconnaissance and security operations to create and preserve options for the joint force commander.[39] Expeditionary maneuver may enable the arrival of follow-on forces and set conditions for subsequent operations.

c. *Develop situational understanding through action.* Army commanders develop an understanding of complex situations in depth, breadth, and context through the integration of intelligence and operations while operating with multiple partners. Future Army forces process, exploit, and analyze information from multiple disciplines and push intelligence to the point of need to maintain advantages over the enemy. Because of limitations associated with human cognition and because much of the information obtained in war is contradictory or false, more information will not equate to better understanding. Future enemies will act to remain indistinguishable from protected populations and infrastructure. Combined arms units possess the mobility, protection, and precision firepower that allow them to fight for understanding and identify opportunities to seize, retain, and exploit the initiative. Army forces possess cross-cultural capabilities that permit them to operate effectively among populations. Army forces as part of joint teams see, fight, learn, and adapt operations across wide areas while maintaining contact with the enemy across land, air, maritime, space, and cyberspace domains.

d. *Conduct joint combined arms operations.* Operations against elusive and capable enemies demand an extension of the concept of combined arms from two or more arms or elements of one service to include the application of joint, interorganizational, and multinational capabilities. Joint combined arms operations create multiple dilemmas for the enemy. Army forces achieve surprise through maneuver across strategic distances and arrival at unexpected locations. Army forces have the mobility, protection, and firepower necessary to strike the enemy from unexpected directions. In high anti-access and area denial environments, dispersion allows future Army forces to evade enemy attacks, deceive the enemy, and achieve surprise. Even when operating dispersed, mobile combined arms teams are able to concentrate rapidly to isolate the enemy, attack critical enemy assets, and seize upon fleeting opportunities. Forces conduct continuous reconnaissance and security operations to seize, retain, and exploit the initiative over the enemy while protecting the force against dangers. During joint combined arms operations Army forces maneuver and project power across all domains to ensure joint force freedom of action and deny the enemy the ability to operate freely across those domains. Army leaders synchronize the efforts of multiple partners across multiple domains to ensure unity of effort.

e. *Sustain high tempo operations.* The Army's ability to sustain operations on land is essential to the Joint Force's ability to implement foreign policy and achieve favorable outcomes consistent with U.S. interests. Army sustainment units integrate efforts with the Joint Force to ensure unimpeded sustainment flows across the land, air, and maritime domains. These units provide supplies and services to the point of need to joint, Army, and multinational forces as well as interorganizational partners to ensure freedom of movement and action. To sustain high tempo operations at the end of long and contested supply lines, units distribute supplies using capabilities that reduce vulnerability to ground interdiction. Army forces operate with reduced logistics demand due to fuel-efficient vehicles and systems, improved reliability, locally generated power and water, and other efforts. Information systems connect the strategic sustainment base to tactical organizations to anticipate needs and provide a high degree of responsiveness and reliability in the supply chain. Every echelon maintains scalable organic sustainment capabilities to preserve freedom of action even if logistical support slows.

f. *Establish and maintain security.* Army forces conduct security operations across wide areas to ensure freedom of movement and action and deny the enemy the ability to disrupt operations. Commanders combine reconnaissance; raids; and offensive, defensive, and stability operations to protect populations, friendly forces, installations, borders, extended infrastructure, and activities critical to mission accomplishment. Army forces integrate with partner military, law enforcement, and civil capabilities to establish and maintain security. Army forces secure wide areas to deny the enemy use of terrain, protect populations, and enable the Joint Force to project power from land into the air, maritime, space, and cyberspace domains. The Army's ability to establish control on land prevents the enemy from disrupting activities and efforts critical to consolidating gains in the wake of successful military operations.

g. *Consolidate gains.* The consolidation of gains is an integral part of armed conflict and is essential to retaining the initiative over determined enemies and adversaries. Enemy organizations operate on physical battlegrounds and in other contested spaces such as perception, criminality, and political subversion. To consolidate gains, Army forces often play a supporting role by reinforcing and integrating the efforts of multiple partners. For example, Army units provide military support to governance, rule of law, and law enforcement. Expanded leader and Soldier competencies allow Army forces to consolidate gains in complex environments. Examples include support to law enforcement and financial actions for intelligence analysts, advanced situational awareness for combat arms, investigative skills for military police, reconstruction skills for engineers, rule of law advising for staff judge advocates, and institutional development for civil affairs officers and leaders within the institutional Army. Conventional and special operations forces work together to understand, influence, or compel human behaviors and perceptions. Army commanders understand cognitive, informational, social, cultural, political, and physical influences affecting human behavior and the mission. Leaders exert influence on key individuals, organizations, and institutions through cooperative and persuasive means. For example, when mission accomplishment requires strengthening partner institutions, Army forces exert influence to convince those partners that undertaking necessary reforms and strengthening critical institutions are in their interest. Emphasis on early and effective consolidation activities as a fundamental part of campaign design enables success and achieves lasting favorable outcomes in the shortest time span.

h. *Respond to and mitigate crises in the homeland.* The Army remains ready to protect the American people and respond to crises in the homeland. The homeland is a unique theater of operations for the Joint Force and the Army. Homeland defense and defense support of civil authorities remain critical missions for the Army as demands on the Army to protect the homeland continue to grow.[40] The Army (active component, Army Reserve, and Army National Guard) fills critical first responder capacity shortfalls to save lives, relieve suffering, protect property, and repair critical infrastructure. Army forces provide command, control, and long duration logistics in response to complex catastrophes or attacks. The Army provides specialized capabilities such as CBRNE response units. During defense support of civil authorities operations, Army leaders at corps and division levels organize teams to support interorganizational partners. Army forces help ensure unity of effort through dual-status commanders who respond to state and national chains of command and lead Army forces operating under the authorities of Titles 10 and 32 U.S. Code.[41]

i. *Ensure institutional and operational synergy.*

(1) The operational Army (those units organized, trained, and equipped to deploy and fight) and the institutional Army (those units responsible for manning, training, equipping, deploying, and ensuring the readiness of all Army forces) work together in support of combatant commanders to build partner capacity and shape regional security consistent with U.S. interests. The institutional Army contributes to operational missions to shape security environments and consolidate gains.

(2) Because of the acceleration of technological change, the institutional Army uses streamlined processes to improve readiness and speed acquisition. New technologies simplify systems and ensure their resiliency in the face of enemy action. The Army works with industry to reduce costs of acquiring and sustaining advanced weapon systems. The institutional Army adapts quickly to changes in the character of warfare with revised institutional training and education for leaders across the Army. Advanced technologies deliver training and education to the point of need using realistic and integrated live, virtual, constructive, and gaming training. Teams build confidence and leaders develop naturalistic decisionmaking skills through realistic virtual experiences and mission rehearsals.[42] The Army improves readiness through streamlined personnel, logistics, and maintenance systems.

(3) The institutional Army optimizes individual and team performance and ensures that the right Soldier is in the right assignment at the right time to contribute to the mission. The institutional Army and operational Army develop competencies in leaders and Soldiers critical to future responsibilities.

j. *Develop innovative leaders and optimize human performance.* Decentralized operations in complex environments require competent leaders and cohesive teams that thrive in conditions of uncertainty. Leaders foster discipline, confidence, and cohesion through innovative, realistic training. Repetitive training combined with self-study, rigorous education in joint and Army institutions, and leader development in units ensures that Army forces thrive in chaotic environments. Army forces gain intellectual advantages over adversaries through cross-cultural competencies and advanced cognitive abilities. Leaders think ahead in time to anticipate opportunities and dangers and take prudent risk to gain and maintain positions of relative advantage over the enemy. Leaders foster trust among other leaders and Soldiers. They develop unit cultures that encourage the exercise of initiative consistent with the philosophy of mission command. Leaders and Soldiers are committed to each other and the Army professional ethic. They remain resilient and preserve their moral character while operating in environments of persistent danger.[43]

3-4. Tenets and core competencies

a. Tenets guide the generation and application of combat power. Commanders use tenets to think about how best to align efforts in time, space, and purpose to achieve campaign objectives. Conducting operations consistent with tenets allows forces to achieve operational overmatch and seize, retain, and exploit the initiative.[44] Future Army commanders consider the following tenets when visualizing, describing, directing, leading, and assessing operations: initiative, simultaneity, depth, adaptability, endurance, lethality, mobility, and innovation.

(1) Initiative. Initiative is assessing a tactical or operational situation and acting to dictate the terms of operations. A force that possesses the initiative renders hostile forces and other key actors incapable of responding effectively or organizing counter efforts. Retaining initiative requires decentralization consistent with the philosophy of mission command, focused commander's intent, and clear concepts of operation. Commanders decentralize combined arms and other capabilities so subordinate units have the resources to act immediately. Commanders accept prudent risk and take action. Commanders encourage subordinates to seize upon fleeting windows of opportunity. Because military operations are a series of temporary conditions, commanders think ahead in time and space to retain and exploit the initiative. Commanders create and, if necessary, reconstitute reserves and other capabilities to preserve the flexibility they need to retain the initiative.

(2) Simultaneity. Simultaneity is the execution of related and mutually supporting tasks at the same time across multiple locations and domains. Operating simultaneously across the land, air, maritime, space, and cyberspace domains allows Army forces to deliver multiple blows to the enemy while reassuring allies and influencing neutrals. The simultaneous application of joint and combined arms capabilities aims to overwhelm the enemy physically and psychologically. Simultaneity extends efforts beyond physical battlefields into other contested spaces such as public perception, political subversion, illicit financing, and criminality.

(3) Depth. Depth is the extension of operations in time and space to prevent enemy forces from recovering from simultaneous efforts. To achieve depth, commanders think ahead in time and determine how to connect tactical and operational objectives to strategic goals. Commanders and staffs anticipate future opportunities and dangers and make decisions that allow their forces to retain and exploit the initiative. For example, because adversaries will use long-range fires, Army forces create and maintain operational depth to protect friendly ports, bases, assembly areas, and lines of communication. Extending operations in time and space applies beyond the physical area of operations on land. For example, Army forces project power from land across the air, maritime, space, and cyberspace domains to ensure joint force freedom of maneuver.

(4) Adaptability. Adaptability is responding to new needs or changes without a loss of functionality. Adaptive leaders possess many different skills and qualities that allow the Army to retain the initiative. Army leaders think critically, are comfortable with ambiguity, accept prudent risk, assess the situation continuously, develop innovative solutions to problems, and remain mentally and physically agile to capitalize on opportunities.[45]

(5) Endurance. Endurance is the ability to sustain efforts for sufficient duration with the capacity necessary to accomplish the mission. Endurance requires the ability to generate, protect, and sustain forces in high tempo operations in austere environments and across wide areas for as long as the commander requires. Resilience, the ability to cope with adversity and losses, is a component of endurance. Endurance often requires uncommitted forces that can operate in depth and sustain operations physically, morally, and psychologically over time.

Army forces also reinforce the capacity of joint, interorganizational, and multinational partners and ensure their ability to sustain efforts for the duration necessary to accomplish the mission.

(6) Lethality. Lethality is the ability to kill or cause physical destruction and is essential to fighting and winning battles. Army forces defeat or destroy opponents quickly with combinations of skilled Soldiers, well-trained teams, and superior weapons. Army leaders seek overmatch in close combat while applying firepower with discipline and discrimination. Precision firepower, effective training, and commitment to Army values allow Soldiers to destroy the enemy while minimizing risk to non-combatants.[46]

(7) Mobility. Mobility is the capability that permits military forces to gain positions of relative advantage, conduct high tempo operations, and concentrate combat power against decisive points while operating dispersed across wide areas. Army forces possess strategic, operational, and tactical mobility. At the strategic and operational levels, joint mobility requires airlift and sealift to move Army forces. When combined with firepower and protection, mobility at the tactical level allows Army units to gain positions of relative advantage and overmatch the enemy in close combat.

(8) Innovation. Innovation is the result of critical and creative thinking and the conversion of new ideas into valued outcomes. Innovation drives the development of new tools or methods that permit Army forces to anticipate future demands, stay ahead of determined enemies, and accomplish the mission. Innovation is particularly important in organizations that develop capabilities as well as those that train, equip, and sustain forces.

b. Core competencies. Core competencies are the Army's strengths, strategic advantages, and essential contributions to the Joint Force. Core competencies provide focus for leader development, force design, and unit training. Understanding and excelling at these core competencies allow Army leaders to contribute to mission success across the range of military operations. The Army core competencies are summarized below.

(1) Shape the security environment. Army forces provide unique capabilities that allow combatant commanders to reassure partners and deter aggression while establishing conditions that support the potential employment of joint forces. These capabilities include special operations forces, regionally aligned forces, and partnered U.S. Army Reserve and Army National Guard forces. Special operations forces provide capabilities that assist partners with internal defense as well as developing the capabilities needed to deter potential enemies. Regionally aligned forces develop relationships with and strengthen partner land forces, share intelligence, increase cultural awareness, and conduct bilateral and multilateral military exercises. Reserve forces, through efforts such as the State Partnership Program, provide unique dual-trained Soldiers who apply special skills from their civilian backgrounds to assist in medical and engineering activities, disaster preparedness, and critical infrastructure and resource protection.[47] Together, these efforts allow the Army to maintain a global landpower network that is critical to preventing conflict and, when necessary, winning wars. While the ability to shape security environments through the threat of punitive action will remain important, Army forces conduct positive actions essential to reassuring allies, influencing neutrals, and dissuading adversaries.

(2) Set the theater. Setting the theater includes actions to establish and maintain the conditions necessary to retain joint force freedom of action. The Army combines forward deployed forces and rotational forces to develop, maintain, and operate the theater structure. Joint forces depend on the Army to provide essential capabilities including logistics, communications, intelligence, long-range fires, and air and missile defense. Future forces will possess offensive capabilities to project power from land into air, maritime, space, and cyberspace domains to establish and maintain vital infrastructure, lines of communication, and protection for successful joint combined arms operations. The Army's ability to set the theater is essential to preventing conflict and, if deterrence fails, allowing the Joint Force to seize the initiative while protecting the force and restricting the enemy's options.

(3) Project national power. Projecting national power is the ability to deploy and sustain land power rapidly and effectively in and from multiple locations and domains. Because war is a political and human competition, the Army provides support to the broad range of political, development, law enforcement, and rule of law efforts necessary to accomplish the mission. Army forces are essential to projecting national power in dangerous environments to secure interorganizational and multinational efforts. Army forces ensure combatant commanders possess the ability to scale-up land forces rapidly through forward positioning, strategic and operational airlift and sealift, and the use of prepositioned equipment and supplies. The Army is the only element of the Joint Force with the capacity to conduct sustained campaign-quality land operations that compel adversaries through the physical occupation of vital terrain and infrastructure and consolidate gains to achieve sustainable outcomes.

(4) Combined arms maneuver in the land, air, maritime, space, and cyberspace domains. Combined arms maneuver is the application of combat power in time and space to defeat enemy ground forces, seize, occupy, and defend land areas and achieve physical, temporal, and psychological advantages over the enemy. Combined arms maneuver aims to seize, retain, and exploit the initiative. Army forces apply combat power from unexpected directions, achieve surprise, and render the enemy unable to respond effectively. Army leaders integrate and synchronize warfighting functions and joint, interorganizational, and multinational capabilities such that they achieve complementary effects. The skills needed to conduct combined arms maneuver across all domains represent the peak of military proficiency.

(5) Wide area security. Wide area security is the application of the elements of combat power to protect populations, forces, infrastructure, and activities to deny the enemy positions of advantage and to consolidate gains in order to retain the initiative. Army forces conduct security tasks to provide the joint force commander with reaction time and maneuver space. Wide area security includes the essential stability tasks including: establish civil security; security force assistance; establish civil control; restore essential services; support governance; and support economic and infrastructure development. Army forces conduct continuous reconnaissance and maintain contact with the enemy to defeat or preempt enemy actions and retain the initiative. Wide area security includes Army employment of long-range precision-strike systems (missiles), high-quality air defenses, cyber capabilities, and long-range artillery and rocket systems to achieve focused control in support of strategic and operational joint force freedom of maneuver.

(6) Cyberspace operations and the land domain. Cyberspace operations are actions at all echelons that generate and exert combat power in and through cyberspace to enable freedom of maneuver and action. The Army as part of the joint team conducts cyberspace operations combined with other nonlethal operations (such as electronic warfare, electromagnetic spectrum operations, and military information support) as well as lethal actions. With Army cyber mission forces, commanders direct offensive cyberspace operations, defensive cyberspace operations, and Department of Defense (DOD) information network operations in time and space. The Army integrates maneuver in cyberspace with the other forms of maneuver to deny the enemy's ability to conduct operations in cyberspace while preserving U.S. freedom of action.

(7) Special operations. Special operations are those operations requiring unique modes of employment, tactical techniques, equipment, and training. Army special operations provide combatant commanders with precise lethal and nonlethal capabilities. The Army conducts special operations, including special warfare and surgical strike operations, in hostile, denied, or politically sensitive environments. These operations may be time sensitive, clandestine, low visibility, and/or high risk. Special operations forces possess uniquely assessed, organized, trained, and equipped capabilities and authorities. Interdependence gained by the right mix of complementary conventional and special operations forces enhances success throughout the range of military operations and all phases of joint operations.

3-5. Conclusion

The Army will remain prepared to protect the homeland, foster security globally, project power, and win. To confront the challenges anticipated in the future operational environment, the Army will maintain high levels of readiness and deliver the capabilities and capacity needed to achieve national security objectives. The Army must invest in and deliver future force capabilities to maintain a competitive advantage against increasingly capable and determined adversaries. Army core competencies and tenets are descriptive in nature and provide guidelines for Army leaders to succeed in dangerous environments while guiding leader development, force design, and unit training. As the starting point for future force development, the AOC requires sustained collaboration and learning across the Army to strike the right balance between current readiness and investment of future capabilities. Only through focused investment and continuous analysis and assessment will the ideas proposed in the AOC manifest as doctrine, organizations, training, materiel, leadership and education, personnel, and facilities (DOTMLPF) solutions that allow the Army to prevent conflict, shape security environments, and win in a complex world.

Chapter 4
Army Operating Concept (AOC) Conclusion

a. Anticipating the demands of future armed conflict requires an understanding of continuities in the nature of war as well as an appreciation for changes in the character of armed conflict. Because technology, strategic guidance, joint concepts, and global and regional security challenges will continue to change over time, this operating concept does not deliver a definitive answer to the problem of future armed conflict. Rather it describes how the Army may provide foundational capabilities to the Joint Force and civil authorities to enable joint operations. The Army under *Force 2025 Maneuvers* will evaluate the ideas contained in this concept and the assumptions on which they are based to ensure that the Army's preparation for the demands of future armed conflict rest on a solid conceptual foundation.

b. Based on strategic guidance and the potential operational environment, the AOC describes how the Army, as part of joint, interorganizational, and multinational teams, employs forces and capabilities in complex environments against increasingly capable opponents to accomplish campaign objectives and protect U.S. national interests. It proposes joint combined arms operations as the conceptual foundation for the Army's future operational approach. This approach envisions the simultaneous employment of forces and capabilities from and into multiple locations, contested spaces, and domains, presenting multiple dilemmas to an enemy, limiting options, and avoiding strengths. The AOC emphasizes the integration of special operations and conventional forces with joint, interorganizational, multinational partners across the land, air, maritime, space, and cyberspace domains. Joint combined arms operations allow the Army to respond quickly and conduct operations of significant scale and duration to accomplish the mission across the range of military operations.

c. Employment of Army forces shows the Nation's commitment to deter conflict and compel enemies in war. The Army's capabilities and capacity provide combatant commanders with multiple options including the ability to conduct prompt and sustained combat or operations on land. As the Army continues to adapt and innovate, it will continue to provide the foundational capabilities that enable the Joint Force to prevent conflict, shape security environments, and win in a complex world.

Appendix A
References

Section I
Required References. Army regulations, Department of the Army (DA) pamphlets, field manuals, Army doctrine publications (ADP), Army doctrine reference publications (ADRP), and DA forms are available at Army Publishing Directorate Home Page http://www.usapa.army.mil TRADOC publications and forms are available at TRADOC Publications at http://www.tradoc.army.mil/tpubs Joint pubs are available on the Joint Electronic Library at http://www.dtic.mil/doctrine/new_pubs/jointpub_operations.htm or https://jdeis.js.mil/jdeis/index.jsp?pindex=0

Capstone Concept for Joint Operations: Joint Force 2020

TP 525-3-0
The U.S. Army Capstone Concept

Section II
Related References

2014 Army Strategic Planning Guidance. (2014). Retrieved from http://www.defense innovationmarketplace.mil/resources/army_strategic_planning_guidance2014.pdf

ADP 1
The Army

ADP 3-0
Unified Land Operations

ADRP 3-0
Unified Land Operations

Allison, G. T., Blackwill, R., et al. (2000, July). America's National Interests. The Commission on America's National Interests. Retrieved from http://belfercenter.ksg.harvard.edu/files/amernatinter.pdf

Army Regulation 71-11
Total Army Analysis (TAA)

Center for Army Lessons Learned. (2010, January 10). Gap Analysis Report # 2-11. Conduct area security over large operational areas to protect against hybrid threats operating among the population in complex terrain. Available by request from the proponent.

Clapper, J. (2014, January 2). Worldwide Threat Assessment of the Intelligence Community [Statement before the Senate Select Committee on Intelligence]. Retrieved from http://www.intelligence.senate.gov/130312/clapper.pdf

Combined Arms Center. (2008, June). Gap Analysis Report No. 08-37. Corps and division joint, interagency, and multinational operations tactics, techniques, and procedures. Available by request from the proponent.

Dempsey, M. (2014, May 14). Address to the Atlantic Council. Retrieved from http://www.atlanticcouncil.org/news/transcripts/transcript-gen-martin-dempsey-at-disrupting-defense

Department of the Army. Memo 10-1. (1997, January 15). Executive Agent responsibilities assigned to the Secretary of the Army.

Developments Concepts and Doctrine Centre (DCDC). UK. Ministry of Defence: Strategic Trends Programme Future Character of Conflict. Retrieved from https://www.gov.uk/government/uploads/system/uploads/attachment_data/file/33685/FCOCReadactedFinalWeb.pdf

DOD. (2014). Annual Report to Congress: Military and Security Development Involving the People's Republic of China 2014. Retrieved from http://www.defense.gov/pubs/2014_DoD_China_Report.pdf

DOD. (2011, February 8). The National Military Strategy of the United States of America: Redefining America's Military Leadership. Retrieved from http://www.jcs.mil/content/files/2011-02/020811084800_2011_NMS_-_08_FEB_2011.pdf

DOD. (2013, February). Strategy for Homeland Defense and Defense Support of Civil Authorities. Retrieved from http://www.defense.gov/news/homelanddefensestrategy.pdf

DOD. (2012, January). Sustaining U.S. Global Leadership: Priorities for 21st Century Defense. Retrieved from http://www.defense.gov/news/Defense_Strategic_Guidance.pdf

DOD Directive (DODD) 5100.01
Functions of the Department of Defense and its major components. Retrieved from http://www.dtic.mil/whs/directives/corres/dir.html

DODD 7045.20
Capability management portfolios. Retrieved from http://www.dtic.mil/whs/directives/corres/dir.html

DOD. (2014, March 4). Quadrennial Defense Review 2014. Washington DC. Retrieved from http://www.defense.gov/qdr/

Essays, UK. (2013, November). Comparative Influence of UK Component Politics Essay #4. Retrieved from http://www.ukessays.com/essays/politics/comparative-influence-of-uk-component-politics-essay.php#ftn4?cref=1

Field Manual 3-06
Urban Operations

Flynn. M. (2014, February 11). Annual Threat Assessment [Statement before the Senate Armed Services Committee] Retrieved from http://www.dia.mil/Portals/27/Documents/News/2014_DIA_SFR_SASC_ATA_FINAL.pdf

Fulton, W., Holliday, J., & Wyer, S. (May, 2013). Iranian Strategy in Syria. [A joint report by American Enterprise Institute's critical threats project & Institute for the Study of War.] Retrieved from http://www.understandingwar.org/sites/default/files/IranianStrategyinSyria-1MAY.pdf

Gaining and Maintaining Access: An Army-Marine Corps Concept. (2012, March). Retrieved from http://www.defenseinnovationmarketplace.mil/resources/Army%20Marine%20Corp%20Gaining%20and%20Maintaining%20Access.pdf

Grygiel, A., & Mitchell, W. (2014, August 28). Limited war is back. *The National Interest*. September-October Issue. Retrieved from http://nationalinterest.org/feature/limited-war-back-11128

Hagel, C. (2014, September 3). [Speech]. Remarks at the Southeastern New England Defense Industry Alliance, Defense Innovation Days. Newport Rhode Island. Retrieved from http://www.defense.gov/speeches/speech.aspx?speechid=1877

Haight, D.B., Laughlin, P.J. & Bergner, K.F. (2012, November) Armored forces: Mobility, protection and precision firepower essential for future. eARMOR. Retrieved from http://www.benning.army.mil/armor/eARMOR/content/issues/2012/NOV_DEC/ Haight_Laughlin_Bergner.html

Hix, W. (2014, February 12). Technology to Enable Strategic Landpower 2025 [Video podcast]. AUSA Winter Symposium-Panel 5 Discussion. Retrieved from http://www.youtube.com/watch?v=QVyukSSxwBc

Jajko, W. (2012, September 19). Strategic surprise. The Institute of World Politics. [News & Publications.] Retrieved from http://www.iwp.edu/news_publications/detail/strategic-surprise

Johnson, D. (2010, April). Military capabilities for hybrid war, insights from the Israel Defense Forces in Lebanon and Gaza. [Occasional paper]. Santa Monica, CA. Retrieved from www.rand.org

Joint and Coalition Operational Analysis Decade of War. Volume I. (2012, June 15). Enduring lessons from the past decade of operations. Retrieved from https://www.intelink.gov/sites/jcoa

Joint Operational Access Concept

Joint Publication 1-02
Department of Defense Dictionary of Military and Associated Terms

Joint Publication 3-0
Joint Operations

Joint Publication 3-08
Interorganizational Coordination During Joint Operations

Joint Publication 5-0
Joint Operation Planning

Manea, O. (2014, March 29). Reflections on the continuities in war and warfare. *Small Wars Journal.* Retrieved from http://smallwarsjournal.com/jrnl/art/reflections-on-the-continuities-in-war-and-warfare

Matlak, R. W. (2014, July). The nightmare years to come? [Institute for National Strategic Studies, Strategic Monograph]. Washington DC, National Defense University Press. Retrieved from http://inss.dodlive.mil/2014/08/15/the-nightmare-years-to-come/

McHugh, J. (2014, June 9). [Memorandum for Under Secretary of the Army]. Implementation of the Army Management Action Group. Washington D.C. Retrieved from http://armypubs.army.mil/epubs/SecArmy_Collection_1.html

McNalley, D. (2014, September 2). Investing in the Army's future. *Army Technology*. Retrieved from http://armytechnology.armylive.dodlive.mil/index.php/2014/09/02/investing-in-the-armys-future/

Miles, D. (2011, May 5). Golden hour initiative pays off in Afghanistan. Armed Forces Press Service. Retrieved from: http://www.army.mil/article/55985/

National Intelligence Council. (2012, December). Global Trends 2030: Alternative Worlds. Retrieved from http://www.dni.gov/index.php/about/organization/national-intelligence-council-global-trends

Obama, B. (2014, May 28) [Speech] Remarks by the President at the United States Military Academy Commencement Ceremony. Retrieved from http://www.whitehouse.gov/the-press-office/2014/05/28/remarks-president-united-states-military-academy-commencement-ceremony

Odierno, R. (2012). Marching Orders, 38th Chief of Staff, Army: America's Force of Decisive Action. Retrieved from http://usarmy.vo.llnwd.net/e2/c/downloads/232478.pdf

Odierno, R. (2013). Marching Orders, 38th Chief of Staff, Army: Waypoint #1. Retrieved from http://usarmy.vo.llnwd.net/e2/c/downloads/280914.pdf

Odierno, R. (2014). Marching Orders, 38th Chief of Staff, Army: Waypoint #2. Retrieved from http://usarmy.vo.llnwd.net/e2/c/downloads/329319.pdf

Pomerantsev, P. (2014, May 5). How Putin is reinventing warfare. *Foreign Policy*. Retrieved from http://www.foreignpolicy.com/articles/2014/05/05/how_putin_is_reinventing_warfare

Quigly, S. L. (2005, October 5). 'Overmatch' is Watchword for Future Joint Force, Admiral Says. American Forces Press Service. Retrieved from http://www.defense.gov/news/newsarticle.aspx?id=17958

Reed, B. J. (2012, October). Leader development, learning agility and the Army Profession. The Land Warfare Papers. The Institute of Land Warfare. (*92*). Retrieved from http://www.ausa.org/publications/ilw/ilw_pubs/landwarfarepapers/Documents/LWP_92_web.pdf

Sauer, J. and Kaiser, M. (2013, August 29). Changing the strategic dialogue: New definitions for landpower and land control. *Small Wars Journal*. Retrieved from http://smallwarsjournal.com/jrnl/art/changing-the-strategic-dialogue-new-definitions-for-landpower-and-land-control

Sauer, J., Stolz, C., and Kaiser, M. (2014, February). Core competencies for an Army of preparation. *Army Magazine*, 41-46. Retrieved from http://www.ausa.org/publications/armymagazine/archive/2014/Documents/02February/Sauer_February2014.pdf

Schelling, T. C. (2008, November 5). *Arms and influence*. (Rev. ed.). [The diplomacy of violence.] The Henry L. Stemson Lectures Series. Yale University Press, 2-6. Retrieved from http://www.amazon.com/Arms-Influence-Preface-Afterword-Lectures/dp/0300143370/ref=pd_sim_b_3?ie=UTF8&refRID=05R6V4RARQ30DNCZ8J09#reader_0300143370

Sergie, M. A., and Johnson, T. (2014, May 5). Backgrounders: Boko Haram. Council on Foreign Relations. Retrieved from http://www.cfr.org/nigeria/boko-haram/p25739

The Landmark Thucydides: *A comprehensive guide to the Peloponnesian War*. (R. Crawley, Trans). R. B. Strassler (ed.). New York: Free Press, 2008.

TRADOC G-2
Operational Environments to 2028: The Strategic Environment for Unified Land Operations

TP 525-3-7
The United States Army Human Dimension Concept

TP 525-8-5
The United States Army Functional Concept for Engagement

TRADOC Regulation 71-20
Concept Development, Capabilities Determination, and Capabilities Integration

TP 71-20-3
The U.S. Army Training and Doctrine Command Concept Development Guide

U.S. Army Center for the Army Profession and Ethic. (2014, July 11). The Army Ethic White Paper. Kansas: Fort Leavenworth. Retrieved from http://cape.army.mil/repository/white-papers/Army-Ethic-White-Paper.pdf

U.S. Army TRADOC Unified Quest Strategic Trends Seminar Event Summary. (2012, December 15). Technology is the most likely game changer in 2030-2040. [Team discussion]. Available upon request from proponent.

U.S. Army TRADOC Unified Quest Strategic Trends Seminar Event Summary. (2012, December 15). Striking the right balance between focused science and technology investment. [Team discussion]. Available upon request from proponent.

U.S. Army Combined Arms Center. (2013, June 12). Army leader development strategy Kansas: Fort Leavenworth. Retrieved from http://usacac.army.mil/cac2/CAL/repository/ALDS5June%202013Record.pdf

von Clausewitz, C. (1976). *On war*. (Ed. and trans. Michael Howard and Peter Paret). NJ: Princeton University Press.

Wilkins, B. P. (2014, May 2). Total Army Analysis. [ARCIC Exclusive Capabilities Development Directorate Feature.] Retrieved from http://www.arcic.army.mil/Articles/cdd-Total-Army-Analysis.aspx

Appendix B
From Concepts to Capabilities: Building the Future Force

B-1. Introduction

Ensuring that future Army forces are prepared to win in a complex world requires a focused, sustained, and collaborative effort across the institutional Army, the operating force, the joint community, industry, academia, and other interorganizational and multinational partners. Future force development must also integrate efforts across doctrine development, organizational design, training, materiel development, leader development and education, personnel management, and investments in facilities. While concepts aligned with the Army's warfighting functions (mission command, intelligence, movement and maneuver, fires, engagement, maneuver support and protection, and sustainment) help identify required capabilities for future Army forces, what is most important is to understand how units and leaders combine capabilities across warfighting functions to accomplish the mission.[48] The Army Warfighting Challenges (AWFCs) provide an analytical framework to integrate efforts across warfighting functions while collaborating with key stakeholders in learning activities, modernization, and future force design.[49] As historian Sir Michael Howard observed, "No matter how clearly one thinks, it is impossible to anticipate precisely the character of future conflict. The key is not to be so far off the mark that it becomes impossible to adjust once that character is revealed."[50] The AWFCs help the Army ensure it does not find itself too far off the mark by asking first order questions, the answers to which will drive development of the future force.[51]

B-2. Linking warfighting challenges to required capabilities

a. The AOC required capabilities are derived from AWFCs. They are the first order capabilities the Army must possess to win in a complex world. Army forces must:

(1) Develop and sustain a high degree of situational understanding while operating in complex environments against determined, adaptive enemy organizations.

(2) Shape and influence security environments, engage key actors, and consolidate gains to achieve sustainable security outcomes.

(3) Provide security force assistance to support policy goals and increase local, regional, and host nation security force capability, capacity, and effectiveness.

(4) Maintain an agile institutional Army that ensures combat effectiveness, supports other services, fulfills DOD and other government agencies' requirements, ensures quality of life for Soldiers and families, and possesses the capability to surge (mobilize) or expand (strategic reserve) the active Army.

(5) Prevent, reduce, eliminate, and mitigate the use and effects of weapons of mass destruction and chemical, biological, radiological, nuclear, and high yield explosives threats and hazards on friendly forces and civilian populations.

(6) Conduct homeland operations to defend the Nation against emerging threats.

(7) Assure uninterrupted access to critical communications and information links (satellite communications; position, navigation, and timing; and intelligence, surveillance, and reconnaissance) when operating in a contested, congested, and competitive environment.

(8) Train Soldiers and leaders to ensure they are prepared to accomplish the mission across the range of military operations while operating in complex environments against determined, adaptive enemy organizations.

(9) Develop resilient Soldiers, adaptive leaders, and cohesive teams committed to the Army professional ethic that are capable of accomplishing the mission in environments of uncertainty and persistent danger.

(10) Develop agile, adaptive, and innovative leaders who thrive in conditions of uncertainty and chaos, and are capable of visualizing, describing, directing, leading, and assessing operations in complex environments and against adaptive enemies.

(11) Conduct effective air-ground combined arms reconnaissance to develop the situation in close contact with the enemy and civilian populations.

(12) Project forces, conduct forcible and early entry, and transition rapidly to offensive operations to ensure access and seize the initiative.

(13) Establish and maintain security across wide areas (wide area security) to protect forces, populations, infrastructure, and activities necessary to shape security environments, consolidate gains, and set conditions for achieving policy goals.

(14) Integrate joint, interorganizational, and multinational partner capabilities and campaigns to ensure unity of effort and accomplish missions across the range of military operations.

(15) Conduct combined arms air-ground maneuver to defeat enemy organizations and accomplish missions in complex operational environments.

(16) Set the theater, provide strategic agility to the Joint Force, and maintain freedom of movement and action during sustained and high tempo operations at the end of extended lines of communication in austere environments.

(17) Coordinate and integrate Army and joint, interorganizational, and multinational fires and conduct targeting across all domains to defeat the enemy and preserve freedom of maneuver and action across the range of military operations.

(18) Deliver fires to defeat the enemy and preserve freedom of maneuver and action across the range of military operations.

(19) Understand, visualize, describe, direct, lead, and assess operations consistent with the philosophy of mission command to seize the initiative over the enemy and accomplish the mission across the range of military operations.

(20) Design Army formations capable of deploying rapidly and operating to achieve missions across the range of military operations.

b. These first order required capabilities are intentionally broad in nature and not all inclusive. Required capabilities within the Army functional concepts derive from and align with the AOC required capabilities.

B-3. Thinking and learning

a. Thinking. Army leaders develop and mature concepts for future armed conflict, assess concepts in experimentation and other learning activities, and use what is learned to drive future force development. Thinking clearly about future armed conflict requires consideration of threats, enemies, and adversaries, anticipated missions, emerging technologies, opportunities to use existing capabilities in new ways, and historical observations and lessons learned. Army leaders develop concepts aligned with each warfighting function (mission command, intelligence, movement and maneuver, fires, engagement, maneuver support and protection, and sustainment) to identify, through experimentation and learning activities, what capabilities are required for the future force to accomplish missions across the range of military operations. What is most important, however, is a refinement of those required capabilities based on an understanding of how Army leaders and units will combine them to accomplish missions.

b. Learning. *Force 2025 Maneuvers* are the physical (experimentation, evaluations, exercises, modeling, simulations, and wargames) and intellectual (studies, analysis, concept, and capabilities development) activities that help leaders integrate future capabilities and develop interim solutions to warfighting challenges. Using the AWFCs as the analytical framework, the Army conducts *Force 2025 Maneuvers* to develop concepts, operational and organizational plans, DOTMLPF solutions, leader and Soldier assessment tools, and policy solutions to achieve the vision of the Army's force in the near- (2014-2020), mid- (2020-2030), and far- (2030-2040) terms. *Force 2025 Maneuvers* allows the Army to translate big ideas (such as, logistics demand reduction; integration of robotics and autonomy-enabled systems; and leader, Soldier, and team optimization) into concrete actions to improve the future force.

B-4. Analysis: Capabilities Needs Analysis (CNA) and Total Army Analysis (TAA)

a. The CNA assesses the current and programmed forces' ability to accomplish the mission.[52] The CNA effort helps leaders identify solution approaches to warfighting challenges, seize opportunities, or close capability gaps. What the current and programmed forces cannot accomplish becomes capability gaps. Analysis helps leaders prioritize those gaps based on risk as well as the benefit that new capabilities provide. CNA assessments inform interim DOTMLPF solutions in the near- (2014-2020), mid- (2020-2030), and far- (2030-2040) terms. Solutions may include doctrine updates, changes in force structure, innovations in training and leader development, new weapons or equipment, and investments in science and technology.

b. The TAA informs how the Army of today becomes the Army of the future.[53] TAA provides the analytical foundation for decisions related to the composition (organizations) and mix (active, Army National Guard, U.S. Army Reserve) of the operational force.[54] TAA begins with a strategy-based requirements analysis using two primary sources: strategic guidance (requirements) and combatant commander operational plans (demands). The TAA also considers Army concepts, first principles for force development (see below), and lessons from *Force 2025 Maneuvers*.[55]

B-5. Implementation: Adapt, evolve, and innovate

a. The CNA informs AWFC interim solution strategies that connect near-term efforts to long-term goals. The Army maintains running estimates for each of the warfighting challenges and revises force development plans based on changes in resources, threat, technology, missions, lessons learned, or opportunities to use existing capabilities in new ways. Army leaders prioritize resources based on how capabilities integrate across warfighting functions and contribute DOTMLPF solutions to warfighting challenges in the near- (2014-2020), mid- (2020-2030), and far- (2030-2040) terms.

(1) Adapt in the near-term (2014-2020). Adaptation is responding to new needs or changes without a loss of functionality. Changing doctrine, policy, leader development, and training may occur quickly and with limited monetary cost. For the Army, adaptation is the modification of existing capabilities or decisions that adjust the balance between force structure, readiness, and modernization. Organizational modifications linked to TAA may also happen quickly to respond to resource constraints as well as shifts in missions and operational environment changes. The Army must adapt faster than enemies and potential adversaries. Army forces will have to develop materiel solutions much faster than in the past due to the ease and speed of technology transfer and adaptation by enemies.

(2) Evolve in the mid-term (2020-2030). Evolution is the gradual development of something into a more complex or better form.[56] The Army evolves using DOD and Army resourcing processes such as the Program Objective Memorandum (POM), long-range investment requirements analysis (LIRA), and the Joint Capabilities Integration and Development System (JCIDS). The Army ensures that materiel solutions are integrated fully with existing capabilities across DOTLPF solutions.

(3) Innovate for the far-term (2030-2040). Innovation is the act or process of introducing something new, or creating new uses for existing designs.[57] Innovation includes applied research. The Army balances near-term requirements with future development investments to support innovation. Army leaders assess what is possible and prioritize promising technologies. The research and development community of practice applies an analytical framework to select a manageable sample of candidate technologies that have potential to address warfighting

challenges and capability gaps. The Army assesses candidate technologies in learning and experimentation activities and pursues mature technologies through the acquisition process or contracting solutions. Less mature, but promising candidates are recommended for additional research or experimentation.

b. Army forums under *Force 2025 and Beyond*. *Force 2025 and Beyond* is the Army's comprehensive effort for changing the Army and improving land power capabilities for the Joint Force. It synchronizes processes and products from concepts to capabilities to implement change. *Force 2025 and Beyond* efforts produce recommendations that help Army leaders direct modernization and force development.

B-6. Keys to success: Future force development first principles

a. To ensure that the future force maintains core competencies and is capable of operating consistent with the tenets in the AOC, the Army uses first principles to prioritize efforts and assist future force development decisions.

b. The following principles may change based on changes in national strategy, joint or Army concepts, senior leader guidance, or the operational environments.

(1) Retain capacity and readiness to accomplish missions that support achieving national objectives.[58]

(2) Build or expand new capabilities to cope with emerging threats or achieve overmatch.[59]

(3) Maintain U.S. Army asymmetrical advantages.

(4) Maintain essential theater foundational and enabling capabilities.

(5) Prioritize organizations and competencies that are most difficult to train and regenerate.

(6) Cut unnecessary overhead to retain fighting capacity and decentralize capabilities whenever possible.

(7) Maintain and expand synergies between the operating force and the institutional Army.

(8) Optimize performance of the Army through a force mix that accentuates relative strengths and mitigates weaknesses of each component.

B-7. Conclusion
Continuous feedback, collaboration, and teamwork are keys to the success of *Force 2025 and Beyond*. Capabilities development efforts drive solutions aligned to AWFCs. These solutions inform Army prioritization and resourcing. Army leaders make force-management and force-development decisions based on analysis and learning activities under *Force 2025 Maneuvers* and apply first principles to evaluate courses of action.

Appendix C
Science and Technology

C-1. Introduction

a. Science and technology helps shape the character of warfare. The U.S. Army's advantage over enemies depends in large measure on advanced technology. The Army achieves overmatch through powerful combinations of leadership, skilled Soldiers, and technology. While the development of advanced technologies is important, the integration of these technologies into Army units and training maximizes the potential of any technology. Increased technological complexity demands that Army forces maintain a high degree of preparedness in peacetime, because it is increasingly difficult to achieve proficiency quickly.

b. The Army recognizes that there are no "silver bullet" technological solutions. The Army retains overmatch through combining technologies and integrating them into changes in organizations, doctrine, leader development, training, and personnel policies. The Army's ability to achieve significant leaps in warfighting efficiency and effectiveness requires an understanding of the interaction of technology with changes in doctrine, organizations, training, and other elements of combat effectiveness.

c. The Army must fit machines to Soldiers rather than the other way around. The Army will pursue advances in human sciences for cognitive, social, and physical development and emphasize engineering psychology and human factors engineering in the design of weapons and equipment.

C-2. Technology focus areas and first principles

a. Because technologies change rapidly and transfer easily, the U.S. military will have to accelerate new technologies into the force to maintain its ability to overmatch enemies. Acceleration requires institutional reform and collaborative efforts among Army, DOD, national research and development communities, industry, academia, and international partners. The following are key technological focus areas.

(1) Mobile protected precision firepower. Science and technology efforts focus on developing lighter weight and lower volume platforms with increased protection and survivability to improve tactical, operational, and strategic mobility and deployability. These new materials, combined with design optimization and new technologies, will reduce overall vehicle weight; increase system mobility, reliability, availability, and maintainability; and reduce sustainment demand of ground vehicles. Reduced support structures enable Army forces to deploy through austere airports and seaports and transition quickly to operations. New materials with improved strength-to-weight ratios, toughness, and ballistic resistance deliver greater protection against lethal and nonlethal threats at significantly lighter weights. Critical to reducing vehicle weight is the development of active protection systems and other technology to increase protection and survivability and counter emerging threats. Mobile protected systems that possess scalable precision firepower and operate with reduced logistical demand are critical

to the future force's ability to project power, conduct joint combined arms maneuver and secure wide areas. The development of unmanned ground combat systems that integrate into manned formations (manned-unmanned teaming) extends the operational reach and increases the capability and agility of units. Science and technology must focus on developing sensors that can locate and identify threats, enable vehicle protection systems to counter those threats, and reduce the likelihood of detection and engagement by the enemy.

(2) Lethality and effects. Science and technology must focus on developing munitions, platforms, sensors, targeting, and mission command systems that provide the commander the ability to overmatch the enemy while employing lethal and nonlethal force with precision and discrimination. The Army enhances formations using manned-unmanned teaming to increase combat effectiveness, expand terrain coverage, and reduce risk to Soldiers while conducting hazardous tasks. The Army develops responsive surface-to-air, air-to-surface, and surface-to-surface fires with extended range and enhanced precision to enable the Joint Force to overcome anti-access and area denial threats and project power from land into the air, maritime, and space domains. Next generation mission command systems are interoperable with allies and allow the synchronization of joint, Army, interorganizational, and multinational efforts. Precision guidance systems improve lethality against moving and stationary targets in the air and on the ground. The development of directed energy capabilities on mobile and fixed platforms holds promise for orders-of-magnitude increases in range, effectiveness, rate of fire, and unlimited munitions stowage.

(3) Logistics optimization. To improve the Army's ability to conduct expeditionary maneuver and sustain high tempo operations at the end of extended supply lines, the Army increases logistical efficiencies and unit self-sufficiency. New technologies enable increased efficiency and reduced demand through lower fuel consumption, decreased waste generation, efficient storage, power and energy generation, and timely and agile logistics and precision resupply. The Army develops technologies to enable automated and autonomous ground and air resupply. These technologies minimize the logistical footprint, reduce risk to Soldiers, and preserve freedom of maneuver and action. Increased reliability, maintainability, and resiliency of vehicles and other systems can reduce force structure requirements as well as logistical demand. Production at the point of need such as water generation on demand, 3D printing, and additive manufacturing reduce the logistical footprint, shorten mean time to repair, increase operational availability, and reduce the need for intermediate staging bases.[60] Advanced and efficient power saving and generation technologies will reduce sustainment and lift requirements. Improved power efficiency, storage, and generation from traditional and renewable sources will provide power under austere conditions.

(4) Army aviation.

(a) Advances in vertical take-off and landing technology improve future vertical lift capabilities and deliver improved range, speed, payload, and performance. Future vertical lift permits Army forces to operate more effectively across wide areas while maintaining mutual support. The capability to transport vehicles and equipment across operational distances will allow future forces to pose the enemy with multiple dilemmas as forces with mobility, protection, and lethality arrive at unexpected locations, bypassing enemy anti-aircraft weapons and strong points. Improved turbine engine, drivetrain, and airfoil technologies keep legacy aircraft effective until future vertical lift fielding. Achieving aircraft operational availability without reliance on augmented maintenance support allows aviation resources to position forward as part of air-powered, combined arms teams. Other technologies applied to Army aircraft will improve the all-weather capabilities of the fleet.

(b) Future mission command systems, flight-planning systems, and cockpit information management systems will enhance situational understanding in air-ground operations through rapid, collaborative mission planning and ease of transfer of mission data and situational updates between air and ground systems.

(c) Science and technology goals for aviation include new aviation assets with twice the range, speed, and endurance of current platforms with increased lethality and protection. The development of heavy lift capabilities would enable strategic mobility and expeditionary maneuver. Science and technology must continue to focus on automation and autonomy to improve the capabilities of UAS and enable the development and fielding of optionally manned systems and manned-unmanned teaming capabilities. Optionally manned platforms must also be more efficient and possess increased reliability to reduce the size of the logistical footprint and allow those platforms to operate out of austere locations alongside ground forces. Self-deployable aircraft will enable increased air and sea transportability.

(d) Technology advances will provide more capable and survivable UAS that have increased commonality and incorporate cognitive aiding capabilities. Advances will provide improved capability for all-weather and global positioning satellite-denied operations. Technology must break the dependency on fixed runways for UAS. Aircraft survivability sensors and equipment, defensive electronic attack, and low observable technologies will improve UAS survivability. Universal control systems will improve flexibility. Advances in technologies to exploit manned-unmanned teaming to combine the inherent strengths of manned and unmanned platforms will produce synergy and overmatch not realized with individual platforms. Aided target detection, tracking, and recognition capabilities will improve UAS capability to achieve enhanced situation understanding, greater lethality, and improved survivability.

(5) Information to decision.

(a) To enable situational understanding across the Joint Force, the Army will continue to develop and field advanced processing and analytic fusion tools, mission command decision aids, and simplified networks resistant to cyber attacks. Science and technology must focus on delivering technologies that empower leaders at the lowest levels with relevant combat information, situational understanding, and access to joint and Army capabilities. These systems must be interoperable with joint, interorganizational, and multinational partners and be designed to improve human cognition and decisionmaking.

(b) Science and technology efforts focus on developing mission command capabilities such as cloud-enabled networks for mobile operations in austere environments and across wide areas. Systems must be simple and resilient, anticipating enemy efforts to disrupt communications.

(c) Information and communications technology such as a common modular chassis and upgraded tactical networking waveforms, must help simplify and integrate operational systems, data centers, computers, and information technology devices. Technologies that mitigate cyber threats will be of increasing importance, as will offensive cyberspace capabilities at the operational and tactical levels.

(6) Human performance optimization. Advances in cognitive, behavioral, and learning sciences will improve critical thinking, increase cognitive and physical performance, foster intuition and social empathy, improve health and stamina, facilitate talent management, enhance leader training, and strengthen unit cohesion. Human performance technologies will help the Army develop adaptive leaders, resilient Soldiers, and cohesive teams that thrive in uncertain, dangerous, and chaotic environments. New pre-accessions tools hold promise for matching a recruit's aptitude to specific military occupations and building effective teams with appropriate combinations of abilities. Blended live, virtual, constructive, and gaming training environments replicate complex operating environments and improve leader and team competence and confidence. Cognitive and physical training techniques could reduce time required for mastery of Soldier and leader skills, abilities, and attributes. Advancements in decision sciences will allow faster, better-informed decisions in an increasingly complex environment.[61] These advances must focus to produce young leaders with the experience, maturity, and judgment previously expected of a more senior and experienced leader.

(7) Medical sciences. Advancements in medical sciences benefit not just Soldiers and the military, but the world as well. For example, innovations in prosthetics technology increase the quality of life for Soldiers and civilians, often returning them to pre-injury activity levels. Improved casualty evacuation and treatment at the point of injury increase the number of 'golden hour' survivors to unprecedented levels.[62] Research in preventative medicine moves the world towards cures for viruses previously untreatable. Traumatic brain injury is at the forefront of both military and civilian medical efforts, with both entities sharing research and technological discoveries. Continued investment in the medical sciences allows improved Soldier resiliency, quicker physical and mental healing, smoother integration back into society, and improved quality of life for the Soldier.

(8) Autonomy-enabled systems. The application of emerging technology creates the potential for affordable, interoperable, autonomous, and semi-autonomous systems that improve the effectiveness of Soldiers and units. Autonomy-enabled systems will deploy as force multipliers at all echelons from the squad to the brigade combat teams. Future robotic technologies and unmanned ground systems (UGS) will augment Soldiers and increase unit capabilities, situational awareness, mobility, and speed of action. Artificial intelligence will enable the deployment of autonomous and semi-autonomous systems with the ability to learn. Decision aids will reduce the cognitive burden and help leaders make rapid decisions. Artificial intelligence may allow robots and automated systems to act with increased autonomy. Robotics will enable the future force by making forces more effective across wider areas, contributing to force protection, and providing increased capabilities to maintain overmatch.

(a) Protection. UGS provide small units with standoff from potentially lethal threats. The proliferation of CBRNE threats will require increased use of robotic technologies to secure the force and civilian populations. The development of autonomous capabilities enhances protection by allowing unmanned systems to operate in areas difficult for humans to access, where threats demand standoff for manned teams, or where the duration of the operation dictates employment of UGS. In the far term, UGS will require development of suitable autonomous or semi-autonomous behaviors, preventing the need for constant Soldier input required in current systems. The ability to assign tasks to UGS and passively control or over-watch multiple assets simultaneously is critical.

(b) Expeditionary. Use of unmanned platforms in mounted and dismounted maneuver formations will lead to smaller, mobile, and transportable manned and unmanned vehicles, enabling greater expeditionary capability. UGS will be deployed to the support battalions to reduce manpower needs in expeditionary environments and conduct routine maintenance and autonomous re-supply operations. Decreasing the Soldier-to-robot controller ratio provides significant gains in unit effectiveness and manpower savings. By designing easily deployable, modular systems with low maintenance demands, robotics add capability options to commanders and reduce support demands as well. Connected to the reporting system and equipped to execute assigned tasks to support the maneuver force, UGS will be integral parts of a support structure that allows commanders to retain the initiative during high tempo decentralized operations. Rapidly deployable UGS capable of establishing mission command systems enables mission command on the move and then transition to offensive operations after initial entry.

(c) Situational understanding. Future autonomous robotic systems help commanders develop and maintain situational understanding by providing persistent surveillance and reconnaissance. Future UGS reconnaissance will employ advanced power supplies to reduce maintenance and sustainment demands. Next generation optics, information, and targeting capabilities will increase standoff. Unmanned systems will allow units to conduct security operations across a wider area for longer durations and enable manned systems to focus on other missions within the unit. Autonomous UGS increase situational understanding in urban environments through reconnaissance and mapping of subterranean systems. Teams of UGS and UAS will execute intelligence, surveillance, and reconnaissance based on tasks given by a single operator. These teams will conduct adaptive, persistent intelligence, surveillance, and reconnaissance for extended durations in areas inaccessible by human operators.

b. The Army is working with joint partners, industry, and key stakeholders developing future force capabilities with the following technological first principles in mind.

(1) Emphasize integration of technology with Soldiers and teams.

(2) Simplify systems and integrate Soldier training into design.

(3) Maximize reliability and reduce life cycle costs.

(4) Design redundant systems that improve effectiveness under conditions of uncertainty.

(5) Develop systems that degrade gracefully.

(6) Maintain foundational knowledge to reduce the opportunity for surprise.

(7) Reduce logistical demands.

(8) Anticipate enemy countermeasures.

(9) Ensure interoperability.

(10) Consider scale and organizational implications.

Appendix D
Risk and Mitigation

D-1. Introduction
Risks to joint and Army forces as the Army implements this concept and develops the future force under *Force 2025 and Beyond* reside in three areas: resources and readiness, technological or strategic surprise, and bureaucracy. The Army must work with the Joint Force and civilian leaders to assess these risks continuously and act to mitigate them.

D-2. Areas of risk

a. Resources and readiness.

(1) Insufficient funding and inadequate capacity (capability with sufficient scale and endurance). Due to reduced budgets, joint and Army forces may not have ready forces in sufficient scale to respond to and resolve crises. Because adversaries will continue to invest in technology to counter or evade U.S. strengths, resource reductions and insufficient force modernization place at risk the U.S. ability to overmatch its opponents. Smaller and less capable adversaries could restrict U.S. military options and impose serious risks to mission and committed forces. The Army may be reduced to a level that puts U.S. war plans and crisis response abilities at significant risk. Efforts to compensate for less forces with precision strike capabilities, special operations forces, and use of allied or partner armies may prove insufficient. To mitigate risks, the Army must maintain high levels of readiness while also investing in future force modernization. The Army must retain sufficient institutional Army capabilities to expand the force. Improved interoperability with joint, interorganizational, and multinational partners provides additional methods to mitigate this risk by improving synergy across all domains and fully realizing the potential of joint combined arms maneuver. The Army must do all it can to preserve fighting capacity in ready combined arms formations while improving the readiness of its reserve components.

(2) Insufficient strategic lift. Diminished service budgets could lead to insufficient investments in the strategic lift necessary to project land forces and conduct effective joint combined arms operations. To mitigate this risk, the Army must work with other services, the

Joint Staff, and combatant commands to identify capability gaps and prioritize efforts to close those gaps. The Army must also prioritize efforts to improve the expeditionary quality of the force through reduced logistics demand and the overall weight and size of the force. Investments in joint vertical lift capabilities with sufficient range, speed, and payload have the potential to allow the Army to conduct mounted vertical maneuver. Low cost opportunities to mitigate risk, such as joint logistics over-the-shore, seabasing, prepositioned equipment and supplies, and other capabilities offer potential solution approaches to ensure the Army remains globally responsive.

(3) Industrial base. The U.S. military relies heavily on private industry to develop, build, and maintain its equipment, weapons systems, and platforms.[63] Decreased demand for military equipment as force structure is reduced and equipment ages leads to a decline in skills and tooling within the industrial base. This loss of skill and tooling could lead to increased cost for advanced capabilities and a decrease in Army buying power in constrained capability portfolios. Because industry anticipates a continued reduction in DOD and Army funding for research, development, testing, and evaluation of potential materiel solutions, traditional industrial partners may shift internal research budgets into other sectors. To mitigate these issues, the Army must work with joint, interorganizational, and multinational partners to provide incentives to industry to maintain production capabilities. Potential methods to maintain the industrial base include ongoing analysis to identify key and fragile industrial base capabilities; sustaining low rate production or making some direct and targeted investment where necessary; encouraging foreign military sales; and ensuring a consistent and credible research, development, testing, and evaluation strategy. In addition, the Army will continue to collaborate with industry and academia to promote science, technology, engineering, and math education as well as identify commercial technologies with military applications.

b. Technological or strategic surprise.

(1) Disruptive technologies. Enemy organizations may attack systems critical for joint and Army operations. The most damaging attacks would disrupt the force's ability to integrate joint combined arms capabilities. To mitigate this risk, the Army develops resilient and hardened systems that degrade gracefully under attack rather than fail catastrophically. The Army and Joint Force develop redundant means for communication and coordination and conduct realistic joint training under degraded communications conditions. Joint and Army forces anticipate countermeasures and pursue a mix of technological and non-technological solutions to build sufficient redundancy and adequate reliability of systems and nodes.

(2) Strategic surprise. Strategic surprise is an "unpredicted development that has a decisive, transformative, and sometimes revolutionary outcome. The nature of strategic surprise is such that it confounds and negates strategy and purpose, not just objectives, but ultimately policy, thereby making irrelevant and futile any follow-on effort."[64] To mitigate strategic surprise, the Army must continue to emphasize adaptability in leaders, units, and institutions that can learn and innovate while fighting. Innovative and adaptive leaders, educated and trained in the Profession of Arms, employ regionally aligned forces to gain and maintain situational understanding and increase their awareness of the changing character of warfare. The Army also mitigates risk through intelligence collection and collaboration, forward positioning of forces in areas vital to U.S. security interests, and prepositioning of equipment and supplies on land and

afloat. The Army's forcible entry capability allows the joint force commander to seize the initiative in response to an unforeseen crisis and counter anti-access and area denial challenges. Ultimately, the Army must be prepared to respond rapidly to arrest the acceleration of events and return an effected area to a level of stability in line with national objectives.

c. Bureaucracy. The DOD is organized as a bureaucracy with rules and procedures, separation of functions, and a hierarchical structure that implements control over programs and budgets. Current processes, including acquisition law, DOD regulations, and service parochialism, hinder the responsive development and fielding of new capabilities and necessary counters to enemy technological advances. Technology change is outpacing the ability of the DOD acquisition system to develop and field capabilities. To mitigate this risk *Force 2025 Maneuvers* will work with joint, interorganizational, and multinational partners to evaluate trends; identify DOTMLPF gaps, opportunities, and solutions; and deliver integrated solutions to the force. The Army will also examine the institutionalization of rapid acquisition and fielding in anticipation of new technological breakthroughs. Furthermore, *Force 2025 Maneuvers* must highlight operational requirements and risk to forces as part of the capabilities development process.

d. The best overall way to reduce risks is to improve the Army's agility as an institution. Army leaders look for opportunities to innovate, overcome obstacles to progress, and take advantage of opportunities to ensure Army forces are prepared to win in a complex world.

Glossary

Section I
Abbreviations

ADP	Army doctrine publication
ADRP	Army doctrine reference publication
AOC	Army Operating Concept
ARCIC	Army Capabilities Integration Center
AWFC	Army warfighting challenges
CBRNE	chemical, biological, radiological, nuclear, and high yield explosive
CNA	capabilities needs analysis
DA	Department of the Army
DOD	Department of Defense
DODD	Department of Defense Directive
DOTMLPF	doctrine, organizations, training, materiel, leadership and education, personnel, and facilities
DPRK	Democratic People's Republic of Korea
ISIL	Islamic State in Iraq and the Levant
JCIDS	Joint Capabilities Integration and Development System
LIRA	long-range investment requirements analysis
POM	program objective memorandum

QDR	Quadrennial Defense Review
TAA	Total Army Analysis
TP	TRADOC Pamphlet
TRADOC	U. S. Army Training and Doctrine Command
UAS	unmanned aerial systems
UGS	unmanned ground systems
U.S.	United States
WMD	weapons of mass destruction

Section II
Terms

anti-access
Those actions and capabilities, usually long-range, designed to prevent an opposing force from entering an operational area (Joint Operational Access Concept).

area denial
Those actions and capabilities, usually of shorter range, designed to limit an opposing force's freedom of action within an operational area (Joint Operational Access Concept).

capability
Ability to achieve a desired effect under specified standards and conditions through a combination of means and ways across DOTMLPF to perform a set of tasks to execute a specified course of action (DODD 7045.20).

conventional forces
Those forces capable of conducting operations using nonnuclear weapons and forces other than designated special operations forces (Joint Publication 3-05).

globally integrated operations
The concept for how the Joint Force prepares for the security environment it will face (Capstone Concept for Joint Operations).

human dimension
The cognitive, physical, and social components of Soldier, Army Civilians, leader, and organizational development and performance essential to raise, prepare, and employ the Army in unified land operations (TP 525-3-7).

interoperability
The ability to operate in synergy in the execution of assigned tasks (Joint Publication 3-0); the condition achieved among communications-electronics systems or items of communications-electronics equipment when information or services can be exchanged directly and satisfactorily between them and/or their users (Joint Publication 6-0).

interorganizational coordination
The interaction that occurs among elements of the DOD, engaged U.S. government agencies; state, territorial, local, and tribal agencies; foreign military forces and government agencies; intergovernmental and nongovernmental organizations (Joint Publication 3-08).

mission command system
The arrangement of personnel, networks, information systems, processes and procedures, and facilities and equipment that enable commander to conduct operations (ADP 6-0).

multinational
Between two or more forces or agencies of two or more nations or coalition partners (Joint Publication 5-0).

power projection
The ability of a nation to apply all or some of its elements of national power - political, economic, informational, or military - to rapidly and effectively deploy and sustain forces in and from multiple dispersed locations to respond to crises, to contribute to deterrence, and to enhance regional stability (Joint Publication 3-35).

space operations
U.S. military space operations are comprised of the following mission areas: space situational awareness, space force enhancement, space support, space control, and space force application (Joint Publication 3-14).

special operations
Operations requiring unique modes of employment, tactical techniques, equipment and training often conducted in hostile, denied, or politically sensitive environments and characterized by one or more of the following: time sensitive, clandestine, low visibility, conducted with and/or through indigenous forces, requiring regional expertise, and/or a high degree of risk (Joint Publication 3-05).

stability mechanism
The primary method through which friendly forces influence civilians to attain conditions that support establishing a lasting, stable peace (ADRP 3-0).

Section III
Special Terms[65]

capacity*
Capability with sufficient scale to accomplish the mission; actual or potential ability to perform.

combined arms*
Synchronized and simultaneous application of arms to achieve an effect greater than, if each arm was used separately or sequentially.

combined arms air-ground teams*
Army forces that merge quickly with other Services and mission partners to form teams capable of integrating efforts across multiple domains, echelons, geographical boundaries, and organizations.

core competency
Those indispensable contributions in terms of capabilities and capacities beyond what other services and defense agencies provide which are fundamental to the Army's ability to maneuver and secure land areas for the Nation.

decentralized
The delegation of authority to subordinates which enables aggressive, independent, and disciplined initiative to develop the situation; seize, retain, and exploit the initiative; and cope with uncertainty to accomplish the mission within the commander's intent (TP 525-3-3).

dispersion
The deliberate or accidental reaction to adversary capabilities to spread out or break up forces, reduce the targetable mass of friendly forces, more effectively cover terrain in an AO, and gain operational and tactical flexibility.

domain
An area of activity within the operating environment (land, air, maritime, space, and cyberspace) in which operations are organized and conducted by components.

element
The integrating functions and activities required from both operational and institutional forces to deliver capabilities.

expeditionary
The ability to deploy task-organized forces on short notice to austere locations, capable of conducting operations immediately upon arrival.

expeditionary maneuver*
The rapid deployment of task-organized combined arms forces able to transition quickly and conduct operations of sufficient scale and ample duration to achieve strategic objectives.

interorganizational*
Elements of U.S. government agencies; state, territorial, local, and tribal agencies; foreign government agencies; intergovernmental, nongovernmental, and commercial organizations. (Does not include forces.)

joint combined arms maneuver*
The synchronized application of two or more arms or elements of one service, along with the application of joint, interorganizational, and multinational capabilities to place the adversary in positions of disadvantage.

joint combined arms operations*
Synchronized, simultaneous, or sequential application of two or more arms or elements of one service, along with joint, interorganizational, and multinational capabilities combined with leadership and education across services to ensure unity of effort and create multiple dilemmas for the enemy to seize, retain, and exploit the initiative.

key capability
A critical DOTMLPF attribute needed to achieve specific success in the execution of a specified course of action.

land domain
The Earth's physical surface located above the high water mark and inclusive of the physical, cultural, social, political, and psychological aspects of human populations that reside upon it.

maneuver support and protection warfighting function
The related tasks and systems that enhance movement and maneuver, and preserve the force and partners.

network
A single, secure, standards-based, versatile infrastructure linked by networked, redundant transport systems, sensors, warfighting and business applications, and services that provide Soldiers and civilians timely and accurate information in any environment, to manage the Army enterprise and enable unified land operations with joint, allied, and interorganizational partners.

operational adaptability
The ability to shape conditions and respond effectively to changing threats and situations with appropriate, flexible, and timely actions.

overmatch
The application of capabilities or unique tactics either directly or indirectly, with the intent to prevent or mitigate opposing forces from using their current or projected equipment or tactics.

project national power*
Ability to deploy and sustain landpower rapidly and effectively in and from multiple locations and domains.

regionally aligned forces
Those Army units assigned to combatant commands, allocated to a combatant command, and those capabilities service retained, combatant command aligned, and prepared by the Army for combatant command missions.

set the theater*
Actions taken to establish and maintain the conditions necessary to seize the initiative and retain freedom of action.

shape the security environment*
Combinations of activities that reassure partners, curtail aggression, and influence local perceptions, while establishing conditions that support the employment of Army forces.

special operations forces–conventional forces interdependence*
The deliberate and mutual reliance by one force on another's inherent capabilities designed to provide complementary and reinforcing effects. Integration and interoperability are subsets of interdependence.

strategic movement*
Act of changing physical location or position to achieve important objectives, goals, or interests.

tenet
A basic truth held by an organization that describes the characteristics of successful operations; the Army's approach to generating and applying combat power.

unified land operations*
Military efforts across the range of military operations to gain and maintain a position of relative advantage to prevent or deter conflict, win in war, and create the conditions for favorable conflict resolution.

*Proposed definition.

Endnotes

[1] Interorganizational includes U.S. government agencies; state, territorial, local, and tribal agencies; foreign government agencies; intergovernmental, nongovernmental, and commercial organizations, as appropriate for the mission. This definition is derived from JP 3-08, June 2011.

[2] The dictionary defines "win" as: to be successful or victorious in (a contest or conflict). Winning in this concept is meeting the policy objectives of the Commander in Chief. It refers to more than simply defeating threat forces; it means meeting national goals and objectives that are unique for each operation. The joint commander must define success for each operation (or campaign) based upon the national goals and objectives, which may change, based on conditions during the operation.

[3] Army foundational capabilities include combat forces, setting the theater, logistics preparation of the battlefield, shaping the security environment, Army support to other services, Executive Agency (EA) (see DA Memo 10-1 for list of EA responsibilities assigned to the Army), lead service responsibilities, and training (running the national and joint readiness training centers). These capabilities are provided across the warfighting functions and include command and control and other activities identified in DOD policy, Army policy, and combatant command operational plans. The list here is not all-inclusive.

[4] A threat is any combination of actors, entities, or forces that have the capability and intent to harm U.S. forces, U.S. national interests, or the homeland. ADRP 3-0, 1-2.

[5] First order is defined as relating to the simplest or most fundamental level of organization, experience, or analysis; primary or immediate.

[6] For example, in a July 2014 Summer Study at the Naval War College, Army forces established and maintained control of critical land areas and used long-range sensors, weapons, and communications to deny enemy access to air, sea, and underwater areas, and preserve freedom of maneuver and action for U.S .and allied forces. These efforts were foundational for Navy and Air Force operations and played an important role in deterring enemy future conflict.

[7] In all cases, unless indicated otherwise, use of the term Army includes the active component, the U.S. Army Reserves, and the Army National Guard. Total Army is not used in the AOC to alleviate confusion. Total Army as defined by some senior leaders includes civilians (the Total Force includes civilians, families, retirees), and the use of the term Army in the AOC is used when applying combat forces (not civilians) where logically required. The Army Total Force Policy, signed by Secretary of the Army John McHugh in September 2012, lends greater official and institutional permanence to fighting as one operational force (reserve and active) providing predictable, recurring, and sustainable capabilities.

[8] Time highlights the uncertainty in war. In the time between conflicts, an army never knows how much time it has to prepare for the next conflict, until the next conflict occurs.

[9] Global Trends 2030: Alternative Worlds (Washington, DC: National Intelligence Council, 2012).

[10] Thucydides. From the Landmark Thucydides: A comprehensive guide to the Peloponnesian War. (R. Crawley, Trans). R. B. Strassler (ed.).

[11] von Clausewitz, C. On War.

[12] Principles of war provide general guidance for conducting missions across the range of military operations and are foundational to Army concepts and doctrine. The principles are mass, objective, offensive, surprise, economy of force, maneuver, unity of command, security, and simplicity. Joint Pub, 3-0, I-2. Since the establishment of the Joint Chiefs of Staff in 1947, joint doctrine recognized the nine principles of war.

[13] QDR 2014, 60.

[14] DODD 5100.01.

[15] DODD 5100.01.

[16] See glossary for capability and capacity definitions.

[17] QDR 2014, 60.

[18] The idea of overmatch was initially described in 2005 as part of Joint Forces Command's lessons-learned efforts. "'Overmatch' is Watchword for Future Joint Force, Admiral Says" retrieved from http://www.defense.gov/news/newsarticle.aspx?id=17958. The discussion of the idea and implications of overmatch continues today. The article "Investing in the Army's future" highlights the need for continued investment in maintaining overmatch (http://armytechnology.armylive.dodlive.mil/index.php/2014/09/02/investing-in-the-armys-future/).

[19] In his September, 2014 remarks at the Southeastern New England Defense Industry Alliance, HON Chuck Hagel, U.S. Secretary of Defense, stated, "[Enemies] are also developing anti-ship, anti-air, counter-space, cyber, electronic warfare, and special operations capabilities that appear designed to counter traditional U.S. military advantages - in particular, the Army's ability to project power."

[20] Clapper, J. Worldwide Threat Assessment, pg. 6, and Matlak, R.,"The Nightmare Years to Come?" Monograph, 3.

[21] Clapper, J., pg 6-7, and Flynn, Annual threat assessment, 14-15.

[22] Global trends 2030, 72.

[23] Global trends 2030, iv and 20.

[24] Field Manual 3-06. Pg 2-5. Identifies multiple dimensions as subsurface, supersurface, and surface.

[25] GEN Martin Dempsey address to Atlantic Council, 14 May 2014. Retrieved from http://www.atlanticcouncil.org/news/transcripts/transcript-gen-martin-dempsey-at-disrupting-defense

[26] DOD, Annual Report to Congress on China 2014, i.

[27] DOD China report, 21.

[28] DOD China report, i.

[29] DOD China report, 21.

[30] Unrestricted warfare is the methods that a country (in this case China) would use to defeat a nation that has superiority over them in arms technology, using a variety of means, such as economic warfare, terrorism and network warfare (hacking and cloning). Unrestricted warfare is a type of warfare that is not limited to war and can be conducted without declaring war, thus 'unrestricted.

[31] DOD China report.

[32] This is the Russian definition of non-linear warfare. Pomerantsev states non-linear warfare includes using indirect intervention through local gangs, with an understanding of the interests of local power brokers; manipulating Western media and policy discourse, using contradictory mixed messages to build alliances with different groups; and using disinformation.

[33] Adventurism is defined as defiance or disregard of accepted standards of behavior.

[34] Global Trends 2030, 72.

[35] "Iranian Strategy in Syria," Executive Summary, Introduction, and 19-23. Retrieved from http://www.understandingwar.org/\sites/default /files/IranianStrategyinSyria-1MAY.pdf

[36] Boko Haram serves as a harbinger of this type of threat. The Council on Foreign Relations recently described this trend using the transition of Boko Haram from an isolated irreligious organization to a regional threat in West Central Africa. Available at http://www.cfr.org/nigeria/boko-haram/p25739

[37] 2014 QDR.

[38] During discussion between DA G-3/5/7 senior leaders: Prepositioned stocks need to transition from the current paradigm of "break glass in case of war" to a resource that supports disaster response and steady state activities, and serves as an indicator of U.S. resolve, creating "activity sets" that more closely supports all missions across the range of military operations.

[39] Army forces will have the ability to change task organizations on the fly and transition fluidly at all levels, as required.

[40] The AOC is consistent with the DOD mandate that defending the homeland is the first priority and one of three strategic pillars. "*Protect the homeland*, to deter and defeat attacks on the United States and to support civil authorities in mitigating the effects of potential attacks and natural disasters." QDR 2014, v and 12.

[41] Title 10 of the United States Code outlines the role of armed forces in the United States Code. It provides the legal basis for the roles, missions and organization of each of the services as well as the United States Department of Defense. Title 32 of the United States Code outlines the role of the United States National Guard in the United States Code. Both are available at http://www.gpo.gov/fdsys/browse/collection UScode.action?collectionCode=USCODE

[42] TRADOC PAM 525-3-7, 24.

[43] To win in a complex world the Army must ensure operations are designed and planned to achieve physical and mental victory over its adversary, while conducting operations consistent with Army values and the Army ethic. The Army Ethic White Paper is available at http://cape.army.mil/repository/white-papers/Army-Ethic-White-Paper.pdf.

[44] In his September, 2014 remarks at the Southeastern New England Defense Industry Alliance, HON Chuck Hagel, U.S. Secretary of Defense, discussed achieving operational overmatch.

[45] Reed, B. Leader development, learning agility and the Army Profession. The Land Warfare Papers. The Institute of Land Warfare. (*92*). Retrieved from http://www.ausa.org/ publications/ilw/ilw_pubs/landwarfarepapers/Documents/LWP_92_web.pdf

[46] Haight, Laughlin, & Bergner. Armored forces: Mobility, protection and precision firepower essential for future. eARMOR. Retrieved from http://www.benning.army.mil/armor/eARMOR/content/issues/2012/NOV_DEC/Haight_Laughlin_Bergner.html

[47] The State Partnership Program links a state's National Guard with the armed forces of a partner nation in a cooperative, mutually beneficial relationship.

[48] The Army Concept Framework contains both functional and leadership-directed concepts. TP 525-8-5, The U.S. Army Functional Concept for Engagement advocates for engagement as a warfighting function.

[49] AWFCs are enduring first order problems, the solutions improving combat effectiveness of current and future forces.

[50] Developments Concepts and Doctrine Centre (DCDC). UK. Sir Michael Howard quotes in the Ministry of Defence: Strategic Trends Programme Future Character of Conflict, 2. Retrieved from https://www.gov.uk/government/uploads/system/uploads/attachment_data/ file/33685/FCOCReadactedFinalWeb.pdf

[51] First order questions are those questions from which all other questions derive.

[52] Current force: The force approved in the Army's annual Command Plan process and codified in the Army master force. The master force includes operating and institutional forces, all Army components, and DA Civilians. Programmed Force: The POM force is the future force available during the Future Years Defense Plan (5 years out). It includes those elements in the current force. The current and programmed forces are described in the annual Army Structure Memorandum, which is the Army's implementation of TAA.

[53] AR 71-11. The POM force is the force recommended and supported by resource requests in the Army POM.

[54] Wilkins, B. The mix includes the active component, Army National Guard, U.S. Army Reserve), Department of the Army Civilians, Contractors trainees, transients, and students. Retrieved from http://www.arcic.army.mil/Articles/cdd-Total-Army-Analysis.aspx

[55] A first principle is a basic assumption not deduced from any other proposition or assumption. For the AOC, the first principles are the set of ideas or ideals from which to base all actions.

[56] Merriam-Webster online dictionary.

[57] Merriam-Webster online dictionary.

[58] ARFORGEN is the Army's readiness cycle and is defined as the structured progression of unit readiness over time, resulting in recurring periods of availability of trained, ready, and cohesive units.

[59] Overmatch is defined in the AOC glossary as, the application of capabilities or unique tactics either directly or indirectly, with the intent to prevent or mitigate opposing forces from using their current or projected equipment or tactics."

[60] Additive manufacturing is defined as the process of joining materials to make objects from 3D model data, usually layer upon layer.

[61] Improvements in decision science foster an understanding of the cognitive, emotional, social, and institutional factors that influence judgment and choice, normative (economic) models of rational choice, and how judgment and decisionmaking can be predicted and/or improved.

[62] Miles, D. "'Golden hour' initiative pays off in Afghanistan." American Forces Press Service.

[63] HON Chuck Hagel, U.S. Secretary of Defense, emphasized the importance of the industrial base in his September 2014 speech at the Southeastern New England Defense Industry Alliance.

[64] Jajko, W. (2012, September 19). Strategic surprise. The Institute of World Politics. Retrieved from http://www.iwp.edu/news_publications/ detail/strategic-surprise

[65] Special terms are those unique to this publication.